ITALIAN PAINTING

KEITH CHRISTIANSEN

ITALIAN PAINTING

Hugh Lauter Levin Associates, Inc.

Distributed by Macmillan Publishing Company, New York

For Teresa and Regina, and my father

Copyright © 1992, Hugh Lauter Levin Associates, Inc.

Design by Nai Chang

Editorial production by Margaret Aspinwall and Mary Smith

Photo research by Ellin Silberblatt and Leslie Carola

Printed in Hong Kong

ISBN 0-88363-971-8

JACKET ILLUSTRATION:
Canaletto
Bacino di San Marco with Bucintoro on Ascension Day, ca. 1729
Oil on canvas, 71⅝ x 102" (182x 259 cm)
Crespi Collection, Milan
Photograph courtesy of SCALA/Art Resource, New York

FRONTISPIECE:
Sandro Botticelli
Primavera (detail), ca. 1478
Tempera on wood, 80 x 124" (203 x 314 cm)
Galleria degli Uffizi, Florence
Photograph courtesy of SCALA/Art Resource, New York

Contents

I.
Defining Italian Painting

Is there any picture more familiar to our image-saturated culture than Botticelli's *Birth of Venus* (see chapter 16), whose protagonist's winsome face, framed by extravagantly thick, strawberry-blond hair, has been used for everything from selling hair conditioner to promoting transatlantic travel? Or Michelangelo's heroically proportioned Adam on the ceiling of the Sistine Chapel, diffidently stretching his hand toward the swift advance of his creator? Or the piquantly androgynous youths who populate so many of Caravaggio's dark, stage-lit canvases, sometimes even assuming the role of an angel (see chapter 10)? Or the calm, sweet nobility of a Madonna by Raphael? These are the familiar, almost ubiquitous landmarks of Italian art, as instantly recognizable as the boot shape of the peninsula itself, and were their imagery, debased through their very popularity, to sum up the achievement of Italian painting, there would be no excuse for this book beyond its auxiliary use as table decoration. Yet, Italian art is as diverse as the geography of the country. At the same moment Botticelli was completing his highly personal re-creation of a celebrated lost masterpiece of antiquity in the rarefied environment of Medicean Florence, in Venice Giovanni Bellini was at work on that all-embracing paean to nature, his *Saint Francis in Ecstasy* (see chapter 9). When Michelangelo frescoed his ideally beautiful Adam, Romanino, working in Lombardy, was making his first experiments in an anti-classical, expressionistic style that took its inspiration from German prints rather than the statues of antiquity (see chapter 10), and in Venice Jacopo de'Barbari had already completed his astonishing trompe l'oeil still life (see chapter 24). Caravaggio's *Rest on the Flight into Egypt* was painted at the same time and in the same city as Annibale Carracci's *Sleeping Venus* (see chapter 16).

No other country offers a comparable wealth and variety of talent extended over so long a time span—approximately two and a half millennia—and in no other place is the familiar thrown into such sharp relief by lesser known works of comparable originality. To those who haunt the churches, palaces, and museums of Italy with an inquisitive eye, the rewards are not unlike those described by Charles Dickens following a two-month stay in Genoa during his Italian trip in 1845: "There seems to be always something to find out. . . . You can lose your way (what a comfort that is when you are idle!) twenty times a day, if you like; and turn up again, under the most unexpected and surprising difficulties. [The city] abounds in the strangest contrasts; things that are picturesque, ugly, mean, magnificent, delightful, and offensive, break upon the view at every turn."

The diversity of the art and culture of Italy—the subject of this book—is a direct function of the fact that for most of its history the peninsula existed not as a political entity but as a geographical area. Only in 27 B.C., long after Rome had become the dominant power in the Mediterranean, did Augustus incorporate the vast, fertile plain north of the Po River as part of the Roman state, and fourteen hundred years passed after the collapse of the Roman Empire before Italy was again united under a single, central authority. During the period that saw the greatest triumphs of Italian art, the country was a patchwork of independent city states, duchies, fiefdoms, and kingdoms, each scheming against the other to increase its power and territory, or simply to safeguard its autonomy. Nor were the divisions merely political. The special character of Venetian culture stems from the close, centuries-long contact the city maintained with the Byzantine Empire in the east, while Naples was successively tied by its rulers to France and Spain: its leading artist in the fifteenth century, Collantonio, was Flemish-trained, while the standard-bearer of Neapolitan painting in the seventeenth century, Jusepe de Ribera, was born in Spain. Milan was in close touch with its neighbors north of the Alps, and late-Gothic Lombard miniature painting found a ready audience in such cultivated French connoisseurs as the duc de Berry. Cultural rivalry led Sienese artists to define their work against that of their Florentine contemporaries, while Bolognese art developed its special flavor in the shadow of its renowned university, the oldest in Europe.

For Dante and Petrarch, a unified Italy was an impossible ideal, the victim of the struggles between pope and Holy Roman emperor, and in the nineteenth century, on the eve of the Risorgimento, even the elementary matter of a common literary language had still not been resolved. In the sixteenth century, the Venetian Pietro Bembo had, with limited success, championed Petrarch's Tuscan as a model, but the matter was only decided (more or less) when, in 1840, the great Lombard author Alessandro Manzoni recast his novel *The Betrothed* (*I promessi sposi*) in Tuscan. If this lack of a clearly defined national identity was true of literature, which so readily jumps political and geographical boundaries, how much more does it apply to the visual arts! It is, indeed, worth asking whether there is such a thing as Italian painting, as opposed to Florentine, Venetian, Lombard, Roman, or Neapolitan (to name only the most conspicuous regional schools).

The regional character of Italian art should never be underestimated. For the early seventeenth-century critic Giovanni Battista Agucchi, there existed four regional schools, which, he noted with evident satisfaction, corresponded to the four styles of painting in ancient Rome. His divisions were a simplification, made in part for the sake of convenience and in part to emphasize the desired analogy of modern Italian painting with that of antiquity. Already in the twelfth and thirteenth centuries, when Florentine art was in its infancy, Pisa and Lucca possessed flourishing schools of painting, and in the fourteenth and fifteenth centuries, the styles of Italian painting varied less according to region than to city or court. Florentine and Venetian art may seem to us to dominate the artistic landscape, but in the fourteenth century it was Sienese painting that enjoyed a European success. Moreover, so far from stamping Italian painting with a uniform imprint, Giotto had the effect of releasing latent energies in the places he worked, whether Assisi, Padua, Rimini, Milan, or Naples. Only in Florence did his towering genius impose itself on a generation of artists, and even there a significant number wriggled free from his austere vision. In the fifteenth century, it is more truthful to speak of the schools of Ferrara, Padua, and Verona than of a north Italian style, and in the sixteenth century, the painting of Bergamo and Brescia was quite distinct from that of Venice, despite the fact that these two Lombard cities were part of the Venetian state. The great court artists of Mantua, Andrea Mantegna and Giulio Romano (one trained in Padua, the other in Rome), exerted an influence on European art far in excess of the political importance of that small marquisate.

Some of these local schools were admittedly of short duration. The golden age of Riminese painting in the fourteenth century—alas, not touched upon in this book—lasted scarcely a generation, but in other instances, a regional identity maintained itself over the course of a century or more, despite the influence of other regional styles. This was true, for example, of Siena, Bergamo and Brescia, Bologna, and Ferrara. That for a short period there existed a school of Camerino, in the Marches, is one of those remarkable wrinkles of Italian painting.

Artists, of course, traveled widely in the Middle Ages and the Renaissance. The case of Giotto has already been mentioned, but no less significant are Gentile da Fabriano, Piero della Francesca, and Perugino in the fifteenth century, Leonardo da Vinci and Raphael in the sixteenth, and Caravaggio and Domenichino in the seventeenth. However, artistic exchange is not the same as a common heritage. The unifying thread in the history of Italian painting is the heritage of Rome. Indeed, the history of Italian painting from the time of Giotto down to the eighteenth century can, in certain respects, be seen as the quest for a lost communal cultural identity (whether such an identity actually existed in antiquity is another matter). The comment of the fourteenth-century Florentine painter Cennino Cennini that Giotto had "changed the profession of painting from Greek back into Latin, and brought it up to date" was a tacit acknowledgment of the Roman roots of Italian culture. It is interesting to note that the geographic area that stood somewhat apart from this quest was the region north of the Po River that had not been touched by the Etruscan civilization, had been incorporated with the Roman state at a late date, and had been the first to break away from the Roman Empire. The Germanic current of naturalism that runs through Lombard painting stems from this dislocation from a Latin culture. Yet even in Lombardy, Roman models exerted their attraction. One has only to take a glance at the portraits of the Bergamasque painter Giovanni Battista Moroni (chapter 17), with their Latin inscriptions and abundant use of Roman props, to appreciate that the hegemony of the humanist movement in the Renaissance represented a step toward the creation of an indigenous, common culture.

There were as many interpretations of this classical heritage as there were regions. In the university city of Padua, the study of ancient culture took an archaeological turn that is evident in the work of Andrea Mantegna, while in Florence there was frequently a more associative, literary attitude to the past. In Venice, Latin and Greek culture combined. Key to an appreciation of these various responses is the fact that classical antiquity was known not only through its visible remains but, above all, through literary sources by which a critical framework for the appreciation of past and present was established.

To a degree that has no parallel in other European countries, Italian painting developed hand in hand with theory. It is this that gives Italian art its uniquely intellectual character and that has made it the crucial force in Western art. The French academy in Paris was patterned on Italian models (as was so much in French culture after 1500), and it was Italian theory that visitors to Rome such as Karel van Mander (whose biographies of Dutch and Flemish artists were patterned on those written half a century earlier by Giorgio Vasari) and Rubens brought back with them, much to the profit of northern painting. Leon Battista Alberti's treatise on painting, the *De pictura*, written in 1435, was unique in its day, and the ideas it put forward—inspired in part by a close reading of such ancient sources as Pliny, Horace, and Cicero—remained in force for four hundred years. They were developed with a decisively idealist bent by the seventeenth-century critic Giovan Pietro Bellori, whose widely read *Lives* were prefaced with a dedication to the founder of the French Academy of Painting and Sculpture, Jean-Baptiste Colbert, Louis XIV's Minister of State.

Part and parcel with the notion of a theory of painting, articulated in various ways by different critics (including Leonardo da Vinci and the Lombard painter-theorist Giovanni Paolo Lomazzo), was the creation of categories of painting, extending from history or narrative painting—the highest task of an artist—through landscape, portrait, genre, and still-life painting. These categories, already implicit in the writings of Pliny, have had an incalculable effect on our ideas about the goals, properties, and limits of painting, and no history of Italian art can omit some discussion of them. The very fact that Futurist painters felt bound to vehemently repudiate these categories (see chapter 27) testifies to their extraordinary power. By the nineteenth century they were, indeed, part of the dogma of academic painting throughout Europe.

This book touches upon some of the regional traits of Italian painting as well as various critical categories. It goes without saying that neither is treated exhaustively, but an attempt has been made to suggest the richness of the panorama of Italian culture. What Piero della Francesca, who was born in Borgo Sansepolcro before it became part of Florentine territory and who worked for the courts of Rimini and Urbino in the Marches, would have thought of his inclusion in a section dealing primarily with Florentine painting (chapter 8), I do not know; the Sienese painters Pietro Lorenzetti and Beccafumi would not have appreciated it. That Correggio and Parmigianino, who both hailed from Parma, here appear with Federico Barocci, a Marchigian painter, is adequate demonstration of the liberties I have felt obliged to take (chapter 11). In this case, the explanation is that Barocci's art is strongly indebted to that of Correggio, which was also the font from which Ludovico and Annibale Carracci drew inspiration for their reform of painting in Bologna in the 1580s.

As a matter of course, a book like this entails certain omissions—both of works of art and of artists. Where, some may ask, are the great medieval Sicilian mosaics? Can there be a history of fourteenth-century Italian painting without a work by Altichiero? How can Neapolitan painting be presented without something by Massimo Stanzione? Where is Genoa and that fascinating, semi-French school that flourished on the Ligurian coast? No less serious omissions will be found in the chapters dealing with the nineteenth and twentieth centuries. My choices have been determined in equal measure by the availability of good-quality transparencies, by the points I wished to make, and by an admittedly personal balance struck between those familiar works anyone has a right to expect in a book of this sort and those without which a certain flavor would have been lost. Numerical limits have also meant that an artist who appears in one chapter may not reappear elsewhere, despite legitimate claims. At times the chapter divisions have favored lesser artists who made major contributions to several areas over those who excelled in one. This is the reason Fra Angelico, one of the greatest religious painters, is represented by only one work, while Giacomo Ceruti, a mediocre painter of altarpieces, but gifted in portraiture and still lifes, and an outstanding master of genre, is represented by two.

Although the book is arranged along roughly chronological lines, I have treated the time span between 1300 and 1800 as a unified period rather than as a succession of styles. Not only is there historical justification for this, but doing so has allowed me the space to create those regional and critical divisions I felt essential.

In writing this book I am indebted especially to Hugh Levin, who first approached me with the project, and to Ellin Silberblatt and Leslie Carola, who have gathered together the transparencies and steered the enterprise through its critical production stages. Margaret Aspinwall has put her fine touch to my rough and blustering manuscript, and Mary Smith has expeditiously seen it through several steps to corrected proofs. Andrea Bayer has tolerantly listened to my endless prattle and called me to task on a number of points. My family has put up with my irritability, and it is my hope that they will find the end product some sort of compensation. The book was written for my daughters, Teresa and Regina—both veteran travelers and the patient companions of what must seem to them all-too-many museum visits—and for my father, in the hope that they will derive some pleasure from its images.

2.
The Heritage of Rome

Painting in Italy before and under Roman rule

Italian painting has so frequently stood at the center stage of Western art that it comes as something of a surprise that it made its debut in a supporting rather than a primary role. Yet such was demonstrably the case. Pliny, our principal Roman source on ancient art, recognized the fact. He readily dismissed the Egyptian claim that painting had been invented by them around 6000 B.C. and thence passed to the Greeks, and he was willing to dispute whether the Greek cities of Sicyon or Corinth could legitimately lay claim to the honor, but his list of outstanding artists leaves little doubt that, by common consent, the greatest masterpieces of ancient painting had been produced by Greek artists in the fifth and fourth centuries B.C.: by Polygnotus, "who first represented women in transparent draperies . . . [and] . . . introduced showing the mouth wide open and displaying the teeth and giving expression to the countenance in place of the primitive rigidity"; by Apollodorus of Athens, "the first artist to give realistic presentation of objects"; by Zeuxis, "who led forward the already not unadventurous paintbrush . . . to great glory"; by Parrhasius, who gave "proportion to painting and . . . vivacity to the expression of the countenance"; and by the divine Apelles, "who surpassed all the painters that preceded and all who were to come after him." Only toward the end of Pliny's narrative, which extends to the middle of the first century A.D., do we hear of a major Latin painter, Studius, who under Augustus "introduced the most attractive fashion of painting walls with pictures of country houses and porticoes and landscape gardens," such as can still be enjoyed among the surviving mural decorations of Pompeii, Herculaneum, and Boscoreale, those resort towns south of Naples that have yielded up such riches ever since they were first excavated in the eighteenth century.

This is not to say that painting came late to Italy. In Pliny's day, there were to be seen in the temples of Ardea, southwest of Rome, "paintings that are older than the city of Rome," whose founding was traditionally set at 754 or 753 B.C. Ironically, the only artist who left his name was a transplanted Greek.

The Etruscans, who arrived in Italy sometime around 1200 B.C., settling in the area that comprises modern Tuscany and Latium, and whose apogee can be placed in the sixth and fifth centuries B.C., have left the most abundant evidence of ancient Italian painting in the form of tomb decorations in Tarquinia and Cerveteri. In the surviving murals, we see an idealized vision of life after death in which the wealthy possessor of the tomb enjoys his favorite sport, whether fishing or hunting birds; is served a lavish banquet, assisted by diminutive servants and slaves; or even indulges in lovemaking. The themes are Etruscan, but they have been visualized in terms derived from Greek art. This is hardly surprising. One hundred fifty miles to the south of Etruria lay the Greek cities of Cumae and Neapolis (modern Naples), and fifty miles farther south, at Paestum, is one of the most beautiful Doric temples to survive (it dates from about 450 B.C.). Moreover, throughout the seventh and sixth centuries B.C., there existed a lively trade between Greece and Etruscan centers, resulting in the wide importation of Attic pottery.

Etruscans had frequent territorial disputes with Greek settlements, and for this reason the Romans encouraged the latter in their own struggle for independence from Etruscan rule, achieved in 510 B.C. The subsequent wholesale adoption by Romans of Greek culture seems to have been even more pervasive than had been the case with the Etruscans, but the earliest Roman painting that survives dates only from the first century B.C., by which time Roman rule extended throughout the Mediterranean. With that expansion, masterpieces of Greek painting were shipped back to Rome on a magnitude surpassed only by Napoleon's looting of Italian treasures following his conquest of the peninsula in the late eighteenth century (see chapter 26). The Greek pictures Pliny describes could all be seen in Rome, and they all perished either in the great conflagration of the city under Nero or with its fall to the Goths in A.D. 410. Among the victims was the famous panel with three superimposed lines, each thinner than the other, painted by Apelles and Protogenes in a contest of technical facility. Its empty, abstract surface must have looked curiously like a Barnett Newman hanging in Caesar's palace. Apelles' image of Venus emerging from the sea—with whose celebrity Botticelli was to vie two thousand years later (see chapter 16)—was placed in the temple of Caesar built by Augustus, while his portrayal of Alexander the Great in his chariot hung in the Forum, with the head of Alexander presumptuously substituted by a depiction of the emperor Claudius.

By the time we encounter the richly decorated interiors of Augustus's house on the Palatine, the villa of his friend Agrippa (Museo Nazionale Romano, Rome), and the various residences in Pompeii, Herculaneum, Boscoreale, and Boscotrecase, ancient painting was in its limelight. Figurative painting had been raised to a level not equaled again until Raphael and Michelangelo, and landscape, still-life, portrait, and genre painting had been fully explored, but these achievements lay in the distant past, separated from the Rome of Augustus by four hundred years. The Romans of the first century A.D. distinguished themselves as collectors, not as sponsors of innovation, and although it is customary to divide Roman painting into four styles, implying some sort of progression, what is really at issue are changes in the way the past was evoked and domesticated by a society whose values steadily increased in refinement and hedonistic pleasures— a society that had more in common with Paris in the Second Empire than with Pericles' Athens or the great days of the Roman Republic. The artists responsible for the fantastical interiors of Pompeii, with their black and red colored panels surrounding vignettes of landscapes or mythological compositions, belonged to large equipages that, as often as not, worked from model or pattern books, probably in the form of papyrus scrolls with colored illustrations. An extravagant patron desirous of the ne plus ultra floor might have reproduced in mosaic Philoxenus's *Battle of Alexander the Great and Darius,* a work that, according to Pliny, held "the highest rank" (one such floor is in the Museo Archeologico Nazionale, Naples). Perhaps comedic pictures were more to your taste? Those of Cresilochus, "which showed Zeus in labor with Dionysus wearing a woman's nightcap and crying like a woman, while goddesses act as midwives" might serve as a point of departure—for these artists did not make simple copies but were fully able, within limits, of evoking the style of various artists, right down to creating Egyptian-style paintings. Pliny records that "great fame has been confined to painters of pictures only" (that is, easel pictures rather than murals), and the elaborate decorative schemes in Pompeian villas served for the display of this type of isolated picture. They were a sort of stage set for displaying the tastes of the occupant. Indeed, when, in the eighteenth century, the Roman frescoes of Pompeii and Herculaneum, buried beneath the volcanic ash of Vesuvius in A.D. 79, first came to light, the painted scenes were excised from their walls for transport back to Naples as the easel pictures from which they traced their descent.

That the Roman paintings that have come down to us are derivative is beyond doubt, for in what is unquestionably the most remarkable ensemble to survive—a room showing Dionysiac initiation rites in the so-called Villa of Mysteries at Pompeii—the various scenes run around the room with no allowance for the corners and the break it imposes on the spatial scheme and the action portrayed. The derivative nature of Roman painting accounts for the fact that the sophisticated architectural schemes employed, no less than the figurative compositions, frequently outstripped the capabilities of the artists, who invariably summarized and simplified in a fashion typical of copyists. Yet this should not keep us from enjoying these sunny, lighthearted works, from which the more profound, emotional world Pliny admired in the work of Polygnotus and Parrhasius have been banished. Seldom has art conspired to create such alluring interiors for the wealthy to while away their leisure hours, perhaps with a scroll of the latest poems of Catullus or Vergil's *Georgics* in hand.

No bedroom provided the setting for sweeter, untroubled dreams than that which once belonged to Publius Fannius Synistor in the royal forest (Boscoreale), built shortly after the middle of the first century B.C. and excavated only in 1900. As in other decorations of the so-called second Pompeian style, illusionistic columns sit atop a feigned wainscoting. But whereas in the Villa of Mysteries a series of cult scenes is shown on the ledge, here the wainscoting, columns, and entablature frame various views of a garden grotto with a grape arbor and fountain; a higgledy piggledy townscape; and an open-air sanctuary. As a further embellishment, a still life of peaches is shown placed on a painted or simulated yellow marble relief.

To the illusionism of the second Pompeian style, the third—initiated under the emperor Augustus—preferred the refined elegance of black or red paneling marked off by attenuated colonnettes and fragile tabernacles that frame isolated paintings or vignettes of flying genii or shepherds in landscapes.

Toward the end of the first quarter of the first century A.D. this consummately aristocratic style was succeeded by one that made of illusionism a virtuoso display of endless vistas through windows and architectural screens, nonetheless always leaving space for some isolated picture, perhaps a ravishing scene of Cupid being punished before the resigned figure of his mother, Aphrodite. In very rare cases, the proprietors might have their features recorded, as in the alluring portrait of Proculus and his wife, their intelligent features surviving the obvious limits of the gifted artisan who recorded them.

To Pliny, who lived long enough to see the evolution of these successive decorative styles (he died in the eruption of Vesuvius that buried Pompeii), it all seemed curiously peripheral to the higher calling of Art, but we may be grateful for these interiors, not only on account of the very real visual pleasures they provide, but also for the glimpse they give of those lost masterpieces of ancient painting that were to haunt all later artists.

Anonymous
Tomb of Hunting and Fishing,
Tarquinia, ca. 500 B.C.
Mural
Tomb, Tarquinia

Anonymous
Portrait of Paquius Proculus
and His Wife, ca. A.D. 62–79
Fresco
Museo Archeologico Nazionale, Naples

Anonymous
Fragment of a Decorative Frieze,
ca. A.D. 62–79
Fresco
Casa dei Vetti, Pompeii

Anonymous
A Garden Scene, bedroom (cubiculum nocturnum)
from the villa of Publius Fannius Synistor at Boscoreale,
ca. 50–40 B.C.
Fresco
The Metropolitan Museum of Art, New York
Rogers Fund, 1903

Anonymous
*A Flagellated Initiate and
a Dancing Bacchante,* ca. 60 B.C.
Fresco
Villa of Mysteries, Pompeii

Anonymous
Aphrodite Punishing Cupid,
1ˢᵗ century A.D.
Fresco
Museo Archeologico Nazionale, Naples

Anonymous
Sacred Landscape, ca. A.D. 63–79
Fresco
Museo Archeologico Nazionale, Naples

3.
The Legacy of Constantine

Early Christian mosaics of the 4th–7th centuries

In the courtyard of Michelangelo's Palazzo dei Conservatori on the Capitoline in Rome, among the fragments of sculpture salvaged from the wreckage of the ancient city, there sits mounted on a pedestal the colossal head of the fourth-century emperor Constantine, his oversized eyes staring out of an implacably impassive face toward some distant vision. Nearby are propped his right hand, its index finger raised in a gesture of command, and his two sandaled feet, of crushing massiveness. Created to dominate the vast interior of the Basilica of Constantine in the Roman Forum, these pieces of a gigantic statue are still capable of inspiring the awe that contemporaries felt in the presence of this larger-than-life person.

Constantine began his career in Britain, at the farthest limits of the Roman Empire, where his father Constantius, a member of the tetrarchy that, under Diocletian, ruled the Empire, was stationed. At Constantius's death in 306, Constantine was proclaimed emperor by his soldiers. Thereby began a six-year struggle with Maxentius for control of the western provinces, culminating in the famous battle of the Milvian Bridge outside Rome. Against superior forces, Constantine led his army to victory under the combined insignia of the pagan Unconquered Sun and the Chi-Rho monogram of Christ which, following a vision, he had ordered to be put on his shields and standards. From this point Constantine's support of Christianity was assured. Not that his devotion to this non-pagan religion was exclusive. He continued to maintain a devotion to the Unconquered Sun and was only baptized on his deathbed. But henceforth Christianity ceased to be a clandestine religious movement subject to periodic persecutions (most notably under Constantine's predecessor Diocletian) and assumed a central position in the life of the Empire.

It was under Constantine's close supervision that the first Church Council was convened at Nicea in 325 to work out a uniform creed (the Nicene Creed), and through Constantine that the Church was enabled to receive bequests and become a landowner (so long as Christianity was an illegal religion, these privileges had been denied). Previously, church services had, of necessity, been held in private houses (an early record of one such service is recorded in the Acts of the Apostles 20:7–10, where it is told how a dozing youth fell out of a window while listening to one of Paul's longer sermons; he was resuscitated by the apostle). Under Constantine, churches acquired a status similar to that previously enjoyed by pagan temples. The church of Saint Peter's that Michelangelo's domed edifice replaced was undertaken by Constantine on the spot where the apostle Peter was reputedly buried: for more than a thousand years it was the greatest edifice in western Christendom. Its construction established the precedent of reusing columns and capitals from ancient temples, a palpable symbol of the pagan world converted to Christ (later, a number of pagan buildings were simply deprived of their idols and rededicated to Christian use: the Parthenon in Athens and the Pantheon in Rome, dedicated to the Madonna in 609, are the most famous instances).

For these new buildings, the costly medium of mosaics was the preferred form of decoration. The tomb of Constantine's daughter, Constantia, located on the Via Nomentana in Rome, beyond the Porta Pia, still preserves the fourth-century mosaic decoration on its vault, in which favored motifs of ancient art have been invested with a Christian significance: children gathering grapes (a eucharistic symbol), peacocks (the bird of the Resurrection), and a variety of vessels (symbols of purity). There is little doubt that the manner in which these motifs are depicted as though scattered at random imitates what had been a type of domestic decoration for pavements.

Christianity had begun as a branch of Judaism in a small province of the Roman Empire in the eastern Mediterranean, but even prior to Constantine's conversion it had made inroads into the highest echelons of society. Saint Paul had known how to make it palatable to potential converts in Antioch, Athens, and Rome, and as it gained a strong foothold in the great cities of the pagan world, it took on a more cosmopolitan character. There were those Christian writers who turned their backs on classical learning, but both Jerome and Augustine—the greatest intellects of early Christianity in the West—had a deep admiration for Cicero and Neoplatonic philosophy, which they passed on to medieval and Renaissance writers. In a similar fashion, the first great age of Christian imagery was fashioned out of the carcass of ancient art. Educated converts had come to recognize a Christian meaning in Aeneas's descent to the underworld, Vergil's fourth *Eclogue,* and the Sibylline Oracles, and the process by which, in mosaics and sculpted reliefs, Christ assumed the features and attributes of Apollo, Zeus, a philosopher, or a shepherd, and angels appeared in the guise of Roman winged victories was a part of its cultural assimilation.

In the late-fourth-century mosaic in Santa Pudenziana in Rome, Christ is shown in the guise of a philosopher-statesman, enthroned with scroll in hand, surrounded by the apostles and the titular saints of the church, Pudentiana and Praxedes, who hold crowns. Although an attempt was made to endow these figures with a weighty presence, the tesserae were used in an impressionistic fashion that disintegrates the forms, and indeed the cross and depiction of a diminutive walled Jerusalem signify that the setting is heaven. Perhaps the most impressive of the surviving early Christian mosaics in Rome is in the apse of the sixth-century church of Saints Cosmas and Damian, which is built into the ruins of Emperor Vespasian's Forum of Peace. Christ appears in the glory of his Second Coming, clothed in a toga, his bearded, Zeus-like features and imperious gesture intended to inspire the awe of an ancient pagan god. The mosaic illustrates a passage in the Gospel of Saint Luke describing "the Son of man coming in a cloud with power and great glory." In keeping with this eschatological meaning, the naturalistic, temporal character of classical art has been transposed into a timeless, semiabstract realm in which the various figures and motifs function both as parts of a narrative and as signs. The six figures who await Christ—Peter and Paul, who present Cosmas and Damian, and Theodore and Pope Felix IV, the builder of the church—assert a historic genealogy as well as symbolically evoke half of the apostolic host. Below this scene, Christ's flock of twelve sheep gaze upward expectantly (the sheep at the sides are restorations, as is the figure of Felix).

During the various persecutions, Christians frequently employed symbols and cryptograms—a fish, the dove, the peacock, the Greek letters forming an acrostic "Jesus Christ Son of God our Savior"—to identify themselves, but the symbolic intent of these early Christian decorations goes well beyond this sort of codified image. Its aesthetic basis is a Neoplatonic view of the world as the imperfect or corrupt reflection of a higher, perfected reality and the belief that Truth is profaned when disclosed directly. In these mysteriously evocative mosaics, the forms of ancient art, freed of their temporal, physical aspect, are made vehicles of timeless, mystical meanings. In the mausoleum of Galla Placidia (the daughter of the emperor of the eastern provinces Theodosius I, and the wife of Alaric the Goth, who had sacked Rome in 410), a figure of Christ, wearing priestly clothes and holding a cross instead of a staff, acts as a heavenly shepherd to six sheep (again, one half the apostolic number, and here symbolic of the flock of the faithful), while in the great church of Sant'Apollinare in Classe, near Ravenna, the apse is transformed into an exegesis on the mystery of Christ's divinity in the guise of a pastoral landscape. The first bishop of Ravenna, his arms raised in the classical gesture of prayer, stands amid his own flock of twelve sheep, thereby asserting the descent of his office from Christ. Above him the Transfiguration is evoked by a cross on a starry field between half-length figures of Moses and Elijah with three sheep/apostles looking on. And above this, twelve more sheep, this time standing for the elect, emerge from walled cities to welcome Christ, shown in a medallion flanked by the symbols of the Evangelists. Various bishops are shown in niches between the windows below. As in the finest hymns of the early Christian poet Venantius Fortunatus (ca. 530–ca. 610), who was educated in Ravenna, these incandescent mosaics speak in a deeply poetic language that is the opposite of didactic: "Earth her joy confesses, clothing her for spring, All fresh gifts returned with her returning King: Bloom in every meadow, leaves on every bough, Speak his sorrow ended, hail his Triumph now. 'Welcome, happy morning!' age to age shall say: Hell today is vanquished, heaven is won today!"

Ravenna, which preserves more early Christian mosaics than any other site, was the capital of a Gothic kingdom from 493 until 540. In the latter year, Emperor Justinian's great general Belisarius brought it under control of the Byzantine Empire (what had formerly been the eastern provinces of the Roman Empire). Justinian sponsored a brilliant building campaign in which imperial splendor and Christianity came together as never before. In Justinian's church of San Vitale, the choir is decorated with sumptuous mosaics showing Justinian and his wife, Theodora—their faces transformed into masks of divine kingship—carrying liturgical vessels for communion, their heads encircled by a halo (who would guess from this that Theodora had been a courtesan before marrying Justinian!). Justinian is accompanied by Bishop Maximian, priests, and soldiers with a shield displaying the emblem of Christ's name such as Constantine had employed, while Theodora is shown with her court entourage. It is a vision of oriental opulence such as was not to be seen again in the West, where the last Roman emperor, Romulus Augustulus, had been deposed in 476 by the barbarian general Odoacer. With that event, the most visible symbol of what had been a world empire centered in Rome passed to the office of the papacy.

OPPOSITE TOP:
Anonymous
Christ in Glory with Saints and Pope Felix IV, ca. 526–530
Mosaic apse
Saints Cosmas and Damian, Rome

OPPOSITE BOTTOM:
Anonymous
Christ as the Good Shepherd, mid-5th century
Mosaic
Mausoleum of Galla Placidia, Ravenna

Anonymous
Empress Theodora and Her Attendants,
2nd quarter of the 6th century
Mosaic
San Vitale, Ravenna

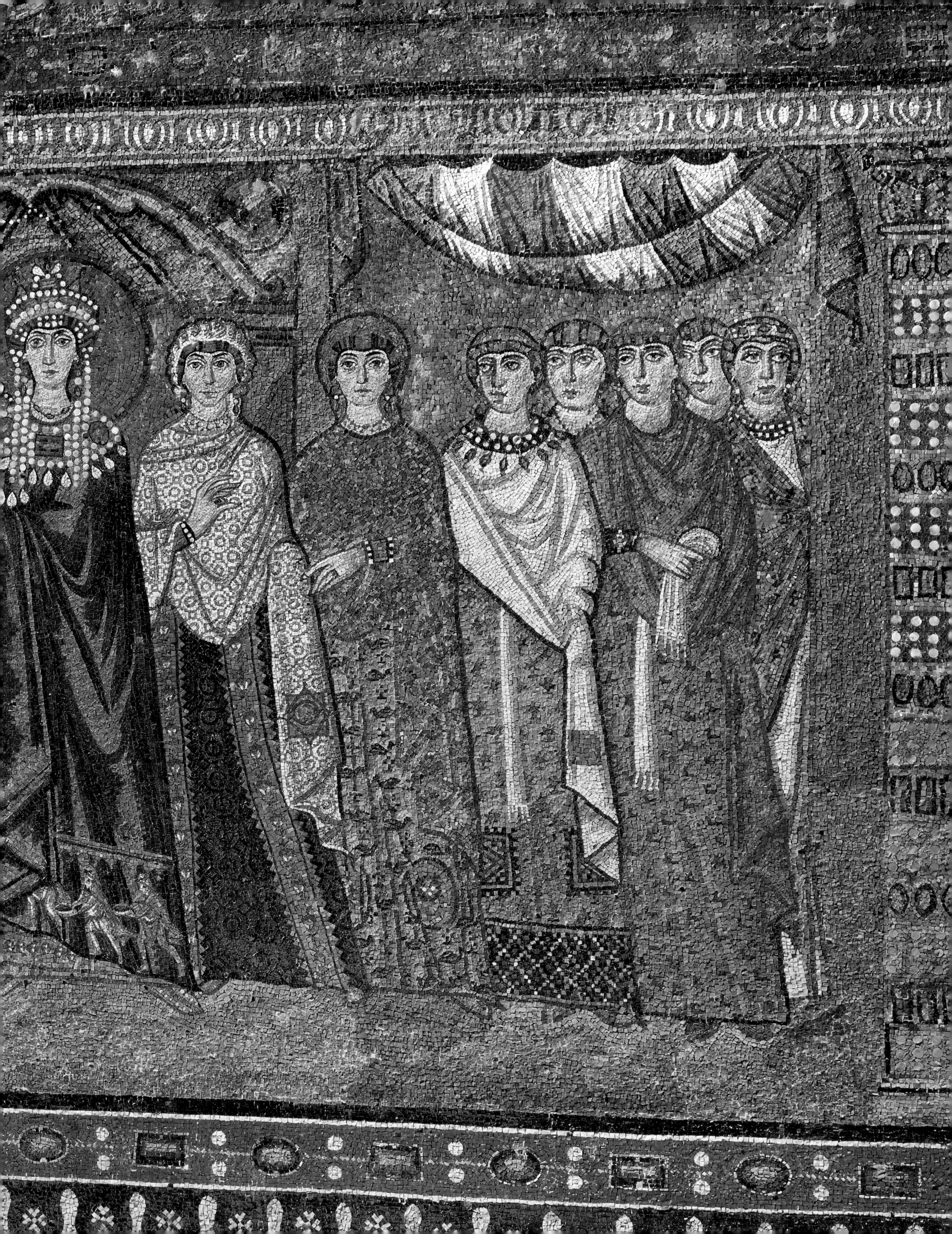

Anonymous
Emperor Justinian and His Court,
2nd quarter of the 6th century
Mosaic
San Vitale, Ravenna

ONFRACTARVINS·NVNCRVI

OPPOSITE:
Anonymous
Apse of Sant'Apollinare in Classe, 6th century
Mosaic
San Apollinare in Classe, Ravenna

Anonymous
Madonna and Child Adored by Pope Paschal I, ca. 820–824
Mosaic
Santa Maria in Domnica, Rome

4.

Visions of Heaven

Medieval mosaics and painting

When Italians speak of the art of the thirteenth, fourteenth, or indeed of the eighteenth and nineteenth centuries, they commonly refer to the *duecento* (or *dugento*), the *trecento,* and the *sette-* and *ottocento*—the two, three, seven, and eight hundreds—thereby neatly disposing of a thousand years. The period stretching from the final collapse of the Roman Empire in the fifth century until the resurgence of civic life in medieval communes in the eleventh is the story of successive invasions, the disintegration of central authority, and a sometimes shocking absence of spiritual leadership from the papacy, which at its low point was reduced to little more than a pawn in the politics of local aristocratic families in Rome. (In 955 John XII was made pope at the age of eighteen through the power of his father; he was deposed for an immoral life by the emperor he crowned, Otto I, and replaced by a layman, Leo VIII who was, in turn, deprived of his office by the vengeful John after Otto had withdrawn from Rome.) The brutally swift Arab conquests of the eighth century brought an end to the classical world, destroying forever the centuries-old Hellenistic culture of North Africa, and transformed the Mediterranean from a Roman lake into a channel of invasion: Sicily became an Arab state in the ninth century, and in 934 Genoa was attacked by Saracens (the event marks the beginnings of Genoese maritime power). The Normans established their brilliant court in Sicily in the eleventh century. In the tenth century northern Italy was under the ostensible rule of the German line of the Holy Roman Empire (inaugurated in 800 with the coronation of Charlemagne by Leo III in Rome). For its part, the Papacy pressed its own territorial claims, based in part on a forged document, the Donation of Constantine, by which the Roman emperor Constantine was purported to have conferred on the pope dominion over all Italy (the falsity of the document was established in the fifteenth century, but by that time papal power was an established fact). Paradoxically, the resulting power vacuum proved a boon to regional or communal governments, creating that patchwork of political divisions that was the basis for the unsurpassed variety and richness of Italian culture in the late Middle Ages and the Renaissance.

Large-scale architectural projects, of course, are dependent on a strong government, and the loss of central authority in the Italian peninsula dealt a harsh blow to the arts. Only with the reappearance of civic life in the eleventh century did this situation begin to change, with new projects for large cathedrals that demanded complex sculptural programs and decorated interiors. Even then, it frequently proved necessary to import skilled labor from Byzantium, whose political and economic might and unbroken ties to the classical past gave it a cultural edge that lasted until the Renaissance. It is arguable that the defining trait of medieval art in Italy was this admiration for the refined culture of the Byzantine court.

When, in 1066, the abbot of the venerable monastery of Monte Cassino decided to rebuild the church founded about 529 by Saint Benedict, he followed the time-sanctioned practice of transporting spoils of ancient columns and marble slabs from ancient sites in Rome, but for the decoration of the interior, he imported mosaicists from Constantinople. And since, as one of the monks noted, "Latin [that is, Italian] masters had left uncultivated the practice of these arts for more than five hundred years . . . the abbot in his wisdom decided that a great number of young monks in the monastery should be thoroughly initiated in these arts in order that their knowledge might not again be lost in Italy. And he selected the most eager artists from his monks to train not only in these arts but in all the arts which employ silver, bronze, iron, glass, ivory, wood, alabaster, and stone." The mosaic decoration at Monte Cassino has not survived, but the fresco cycle in the dependency of Sant'Angelo in Formis, near Capua, gives an idea of their splendor.

In Norman Sicily, Roger II followed the same practice, importing Byzantine craftsmen to decorate his palace chapel erected in Palermo between 1132 and 1140. Over the next half century, Greek mosaicists and those trained under them carried out extensive decorative cycles of unsurpassed majesty in Palermo, Monreale, and Cefalù. We hear of Greek masters in Ravenna in 1112 and in Ferrara in 1135.

Venice inherited a certain technical knowledge of mosaic practice from the Byzantine exarchate at Ravenna, but in 1153 there is notice of a Greek mosaicist, Marcus Grecus, in the city, and there can be no doubt that close ties to the Byzantine Empire were responsible for the high level of technical proficiency exhibited by the mosaics in the doge's church of San Marco, created in emulation of the Hagia Sophia in Constantinople. In 1258 an edict was issued in Venice providing that every master of mosaics had to train at least two apprentices, with the result that by the thirteenth century Venetian artisans had acquired a deserved fame. Those mosaicists who later worked in Pisa and Florence were Venetian-trained.

It was not simply the technique of mosaics but the actual decorative programs of Byzantine churches that were adopted. The classical Byzantine program incorporated an image of the Virgin in the apse and a bust-length figure of Christ—the Pantocrator—in the central dome. In the Sicilian churches at Cefalù and Monreale, monumental depictions of the Pantocrator fill the curved surface of the apse, while in the cathedral of Torcello, in the Venetian Lagoon, a standing figure of the Virgin holding the Christ Child is shown. Following the defeat of Constantinople by Western powers in 1204, Venetians brought back columns, marble, and mosaic material for the decoration of San Marco. They also looted libraries, and the decorative scheme of one of the domes in the narthex of San Marco is based on a late-fifth-century Greek manuscript of the book of Genesis.

Perhaps nowhere is the Byzantine basis of Venetian art more beautifully demonstrated than in the thirteenth-century mosaic of the Madonna and Child in the cathedral of Torcello. The Virgin, whose head is flanked by the Greek letters for "Mother of God," follows the Byzantine formula known as the *Hodegetria:* the Virgin gestures to her son, who holds his scroll like an infant teacher and raises his right hand in blessing. However, so far from being the stiff image often encountered elsewhere, she bends one leg in a contrapposto stance that can be traced back to ancient images of Venus.

The apse decorations of early Christian churches had frequently evoked a richly planted, paradisiacal garden or a vision of a cloud-streaked sky (see chapter 3). Medieval art, with its even more pronounced eschatological bent, replaced this allusively earthly setting with a gold empyrean that removed the figures from any recognizable realm to a heavenly vision. Disembodied through an abstracting instinct that reduced the human form to a pose or gesture and interpreted drapery folds as pattern, the figures were meant to have a timeless quality reflecting the sanctity of the holy personages depicted rather than plausibly re-creating their worldly appearance.

There can be little question that Greek models also stand behind many of the altarpieces and crucifixes produced at this time: however much these works may differ according to the region in which they were produced, the fourteenth-century painter Cennino Cennini was perfectly correct to refer to their style as the "maniera greca." Without Byzantine models it is doubtful whether the Tuscan Berlinghiero Berlinghieri, who was from Lucca, could have arrived at the suave, almost feminine beauty of his hypnotic crucifix, in which the figure of Christ, his eyes directed to the worshiper, seems mystically suspended before the blue field of the cross, his triumph over death implicit in his psychological detachment. At the sides, on the gilt aprons, are shown diminutive figures of the mourning Virgin and Saint John, while the terminals are decorated with the four symbols of the Evangelists, the Virgin flanked by two angels, and a scene of the denial of Peter—a mixture of apocalyptic vision and biblical narrative. This manner of treating the Crucifixion in an allusive fashion can be traced to early Christian prototypes, when it was thought unseemly to show the Son of God dead. By the middle of the thirteenth century a new type of crucifix had emerged in which Christ hangs from the cross, his body describing an arc of pathos. This formula reached its peak of emotional urgency in the hands of Giunto Pisano and Cimabue, and its adoption marks a coming of age of Western painting.

Understandably, the place most resistant to Greek models was Rome, where the examples of early Christian art were near at hand. In the twelfth-century mosaic in the apse of San Clemente, the figure of the crucified Christ (far less elegant than that of Berlinghiero) is shown against a gold background overlaid with the heavy tendrils of acanthus vines interspersed with flowers, birds, winged children, and bookish monks. But it was in the thirteenth century that artists first asserted their claim to being the heirs of an indigenous Roman culture. In the awe-inspiring mosaic decoration in the apse of Santa Maria Maggiore to which Jacopo Torriti put his name in 1295, the Virgin's coronation in heaven has been conceived as the reenactment of a splendidly imperial ceremony. The figures, of a gravity and weight that marks a new chapter in Western art, are seated on a jewel-encrusted throne set into a starry field. Once again, the gold background is enlivened by acanthus vines derived from classical sarcophagi or the decorations of an ancient marble doorframe. Before this almost palpably real vision, angels mark out their own space. Quite apart from the contact Jacopo Torriti had probably already had with the revolutionary art of Giotto, the example of the fifth-century mosaics in the nave of Santa Maria Maggiore must be reckoned as a primary source of inspiration. In the late 1270s Torriti's compatriot Pietro Cavallini worked on a cycle of frescoes in the early Christian basilica of San Paolo fuori le Mura, in which his task was partly to restore a preexistent, probably fifth-century cycle, and partly to create anew. The cycle is destroyed, but in the Last Judgment he painted on the entrance wall of the church of Santa Cecilia, the open links of the chain binding medieval to ancient art were closed, and any dependency on Byzantine prototypes superseded.

As Pietro Cavallini's art eloquently demonstrates, the purposely hieratic and abstract quality of medieval art had an afterlife. It is, for example, evident in Giusto de'Menabuoi's use of ritualistic gesture in his frescoes on the vault of the baptistery of Padua, where the heads of the cherubim and seraphim are arranged in a repeating pattern of concentric circles around an austere figure of Christ. This work was painted seventy years after Giotto had transformed the interior of the Arena Chapel, just a short distance away, with a cycle of frescoes that redirected painting from the fixed forms of medieval art to the changeable, transitory experience of the world around us.

Anonymous
Virgin, 13th century
Mosaic
Cathedral, Torcello

MARIA VIRGO ASSVPTA E AD ETHEREV ThALAMV IN QVO REX REGV STELLATO SEDET SOLIO

Pietro Cavallini (active 1250–ca. 1330)
Christ in Glory, ca. 1293
Fresco
Santa Cecilia, Rome

OPPOSITE:
Jacopo Torriti (active late 13ᵗʰ century)
Coronation of the Virgin, ca. 1295
Mosaic
Santa Maria Maggiore, Rome

Berlinghiero Berlinghieri
(active by 1228, died by 1236)
Crucifix, ca. 1230–35
Tempera and gold on wood,
68⅞ x 55⅛" (175 x 140 cm)
Museo Nazionale
di Villa Guinigi, Lucca

Anonymous
*Madonna and Child (The Madonna
del Fulmine)*, 13th century
Tempera and gold on wood,
78¾ x 35" (200 x 89 cm)
Museo Nazionale di Capodimonte, Naples

37

5.

Sermons in Paint

Religious painting in the age of Saint Francis and Giotto

Toward the end of his life, in 1223, Saint Francis determined to celebrate Christmas in a fashion that would bring the event alive to his audience. For the occasion he chose a cave-riddled hill opposite the village of Greccio, northeast of Rome, that was owned by Giovanni Velita, the local lord and a devoted follower. After obtaining papal consent for his proposed innovations, Francis arranged with Velita to have an ox, an ass, and a manger set up beneath a shelter, together with an altar for the celebration of mass. There, by candlelight, accompanied by the chants of fellow monks, he delivered a moving homily on the humility and sufferings of Christ in words so sweet that Velita attested he saw the Christ Child appear on a bed of hay, awaken, and smile at the saint.

Few would count this among Saint Francis's most memorable miracles, but it is emblematic both of the populist nature of his ministry and of his keen appreciation for what we would call visual aids. Saint Francis knew well the power of images: he had first heard the voice of God while praying before a painted crucifix in a dilapidated church outside Assisi.

Fittingly, it was in the service of the two great preaching orders founded in the early thirteenth century—the Franciscans and the Dominicans—that the potential of painting as an instrument of persuasion rather than of simple instruction was first realized. Saint Francis had opposed the ownership of property, preferring the Apostolic virtue of poverty, but this was unworkable once the Franciscan order spread and became the recipient of vast gifts and bequests. The double-story church built in honor of Saint Francis on the slopes of his native Assisi is both a masterpiece of Gothic engineering and the most extensively decorated church in Europe. Every available wall space is given over to fresco cycles detailing the Creation, the life of Christ and his Passion, the lives of various saints, and, of course, the life of Saint Francis. There is no question but that Francis, who at his death insisted on being laid on the ground wearing borrowed clothes, would have disapproved of such a sanctuary. Nonetheless, the images on its walls have provided instruction and consolation to millions of pilgrims and visitors.

What makes these frescoes so remarkable is not their extensiveness, but the caliber of the artists who were hired to paint them—Cimabue, Giotto, Pietro Lorenzetti, and Simone Martini— and the innovative style employed. It is in the basilica of San Francesco at Assisi that European painting first took as its frame of reference the world of experience rather than a theological ideal. In the hands of Giotto and his followers, Saint Francis was no longer shown as a conventionalized, medieval ascetic, as he had appeared in those altarpieces made shortly after his death in 1226 and his canonization in 1228. He took on the weighty, three-dimensional aspect of a real person inhabiting solidly built cities and compact landscapes resembling those of central Italy. In the scene of Saint Francis preaching to the birds, in which Francis's solemn companion raises his hand in mild surprise at the attentiveness a noisy flock of birds accords an impromptu sermon, the very manner in which some birds were shown in mid flight was a tour de force of representation.

This new art, created by Giotto in the 1290s, spread quickly throughout Italy and gave new authority to sacred stories and legends. The subject might be the apocryphal account of the disgraced Joachim reunited with his aged wife, Anne, before the Golden Gate of Jerusalem, treated by Giotto with an unprecedented eye to those outward signs of human tenderness, in the Arena Chapel in Padua. Or it might be an event of the recent past, such as one Ambrogio Lorenzetti depicted in a fresco in the church of San Francesco in Siena, showing Saint Louis of Toulouse kneeling before Pope Boniface VIII, whose court, backed by a row of social dandies, buzzes with the news of the holy man's renunciation of his worldly position to become a Franciscan friar.

This newfound ability to create visual sermons, with the vividly descriptive language of a medieval preacher, was exploited for a variety of tasks. In Taddeo Gaddi's frescoes on the end wall of the refectory of Santa Croce in Florence, the monks eating their meals could look up to a depiction of the Last Supper that seemed to project into the space of the room, compelling them to accept Christ as their host. Or they could glance higher and see their founder, Saint Francis, embracing the mystical tree of life on which Christ is shown crucified. Murals such as this became an obligatory devotional aid to monks: those painted later by Andrea del Castagno, Domenico Ghirlandaio, Perugino, Andrea del Sarto, and Leonardo da Vinci might employ more audacious perspectival settings and a more realistic vocabulary, but the means are essentially the same as Taddeo's.

Not for a thousand years had it been possible to make the torments of Hell, the consequences of a life given over to hedonistic pleasure, or the apocalyptic vision of the end of time appear as plausible eventualities rather than abstract threats. Such scenes were painted where they would have the greatest effect, in a private funerary chapel or on the walls of a cemetery or cloister. The new art—in myriad variations—was especially effective in making vivid the lives of recently deceased saints and their ability to intervene on behalf of their devotees. In Simone Martini's painting of the Augustinian monk, the Blessed Agostino Novello, a full-length image of the saint standing amid the trees of his favorite wooded retreat is flanked by depictions of him performing a variety of miracles, including the rescue of a child who has fallen from a balcony and the resuscitation of an infant mauled by a dog. Grimacing cripples eagerly press around the Franciscan Blessed Filippino Ciardella in a piece of fourteenth-century *verismo* by that crude Sienese populist Bartolo di Fredi, while some seventy years later Giovanni di Paolo turned his more eccentric gifts to evoking the magical intervention of Saint Nicholas of Tolentino, hovering over a surreal vision of a storm-tossed ship (a mermaid, emblematic of imminent danger, slips silently away through the waves). The character and power of these scenes depended as much on the audience addressed as on the figure whose life was commemorated. Simone's altarpiece was for the urban population of Siena, where it adorned the Blessed Agostino Novello's tomb, while Bartolo di Fredi's scene was for the provincial town of Montalcino, south of Siena. Sano di Pietro's matter-of-fact portrayal of the fifteenth-century revivalist preacher Saint Bernardino before the Palazzo Pubblico was painted for a lay confraternity whose members had known the saint personally and expected a piece of reportage rather than an embellished legend: every effort has been made to re-create the event accurately, right down to the division between male and female listeners.

Just as remarkable was the use to which the new art was put as an instrument of meditation. The sublime image of Saint Francis borne across the ocean like a second Christ appearing at dawn, painted by the fifteenth-century Sienese Sassetta, is from the reverse of a large, double-sided altarpiece and was the focus of the Franciscan friars saying their offices in the choir of their church in Borgo Sansepolcro in Tuscany (it is now dismantled and its parts scattered). Fra Angelico's scene of the Annunciation adorns a cell in the Dominican monastery of San Marco in Florence. It includes a devout figure of Saint Peter Martyr, his hands reverently clasped, as an inducement to the isolated meditation of its occupant.

In the seventeenth century, the Jesuits were to reaffirm the use of art as an instrument of persuasion, but the theatrically bombastic images they sometimes employed, however remarkable both as works of art and as propaganda, were a far cry from the simple, affective pictures of the age of Saint Francis and his followers.

OPPOSITE:
Giotto (1266–1337)
Saint Francis Preaching to the Birds, 1290s
Fresco
Upper Church of San Francesco, Assisi

Giotto (1266–1337)
The Meeting at the Golden Gate, ca. 1304–6
Fresco
Arena Chapel (Cappella degli Scrovegni), Padua

PAGE 42:
Taddeo Gaddi (ca. 1300–1366)
Christ Crucified on the Mystical Tree of Life, ca. 1360
Fresco
Refectory of Santa Croce, Florence

PAGE 43, TOP:
Simone Martini (active by 1315, died 1344)
Altarpiece of Beato Agostino Novello, ca. 1326
Tempera and gold on wood,
78¾ x 100¾" (200 x 256 cm)
Pinacoteca Nazionale, Siena

PAGE 43, BOTTOM:
Sassetta (1392–1450)
Saint Francis in Glory, with the Virtues and Vices,
with Blessed Reinieri and Saint John the Baptist, 1437–44
Tempera and gold on wood,
81½ x 46½" (207 x 118 cm)
Harvard University Center for Renaissance
Studies, Villa I Tatti, Florence

41

42

43

Bartolo di Fredi (active by 1353, died 1410)
Blessed Filippino Ciardella Healing a Cripple, 1382
Tempera and gold on wood
31⅞ x 27½" (81 x 70 cm)
Museo Civico, Montalcino

OPPOSITE:
Giovanni di Paolo (active by 1417, died 1482)
Saint Nicholas of Tolentino Intervenes to Save Sailors, 1356
Tempera and gold on wood, 20½ x 16⅝" (52 x 42.3 cm)
Philadelphia Museum of Art
The John G. Johnson Collection

44

Fra Angelico (active by 1417, died 1455)
The Annunciation with Saint Peter Martyr, ca. 1440–47
Fresco
Museo di San Marco, Florence

OPPOSITE:
Sano di Pietro (1406–1481)
Saint Bernardino Preaching before the Palazzo Pubblico of Siena, ca. 1448
Tempera and gold on wood, 64⅛ x 40⅛" (163 x 102 cm)
Sala Capitolare, Cathedral, Siena

6.
Painting for the Medieval Commune

Civic commissions in the late Middle Ages

The division between Church and State that we are today so careful to maintain would have struck the inhabitant of a city or commune in the thirteenth–sixteenth centuries as nothing short of absurd. The welfare of his city depended on divine favor as much as on sound government. Indeed, good government itself was mandated by God.

We may look upon the great painting of the Virgin in majesty—the *Maestà*—completed by Duccio in 1311 for the cathedral of Siena as an exalted religious icon, but the inscription that adorns the Madonna's throne carries a civic as well as a personal supplication: "O Mother of God, may you be to Siena peace and life to Duccio, who painted you thus." Duccio's altarpiece was commissioned as a replacement for an outdated image of the Virgin that, in turn, had replaced a still earlier, highly venerated painting before which the population of the city had prayed for protection when threatened by defeat at the hands of the Florentines in 1260. Thereafter, an annual procession to the altar of the Virgin was held at which representatives of the Sienese state renewed their vow made on that occasion. An image of the Virgin was on the seal of the city, and in 1315 Simone Martini painted a monumental fresco of her in the main chamber of the city hall, below which runs an inscription urging the rulers of Siena to govern justly.

In Florence, Saint John the Baptist, not the Virgin, was the patron saint. However, in the old grain market of Orsanmichele, situated midway between the Palazzo Vecchio and the cathedral, there was a miraculous image of the Madonna, and when, in 1336, the city council decided to erect a new building, it was a matter of course that a picture of the Madonna and Child should be commissioned and given a place of honor. The task was entrusted to Bernardo Daddi, who in 1347 painted the large *Madonna delle Grazie* that still adorns the altar. The oratory of Orsanmichele is below what used to be the vast storeroom of the city's granary, and Daddi's painting owed its venerable status both to the miraculous image it replaced and to its placement in this most important civic building, whose decorations were the responsibility of the leading guilds of Florence.

Carlo Crivelli's sumptuously detailed *Annunciation* may, at first glance, appear an unlikely candidate for a communal subject, but it commemorates the fact that the citizens of Ascoli Piceno were granted certain liberties by the Church on the Feast of the Annunciation, on March 25, 1482. Thereafter, an annual procession was made to the altar. It is for this reason that the painting bears the inscription "Ecclesiastical Liberty" together with the arms of the bishop of Ascoli, of Pope Innocent VIII, and of the city of Ascoli, and it is for this reason that the city's patron saint, shown holding a model of the city, accompanies the Archangel Gabriel on his divine mission.

Even Piero della Francesca's fresco of the risen Christ, solemnly standing in his tomb surrounded by sleeping soldiers in the silence of Easter Morning, is a communal image in the former city hall of Borgo Sansepolcro. The city traced its origins to pilgrims returning from

Palestine with relics of the Holy Sepulcher (whence the name of the city), and a figure of the resurrected Christ became the emblem of the city.

Just as peculiar to us is the presence of what we would consider secular images in churches: Paolo Uccello's fresco commemorating the Florentine Captain Sir John Hawkwood, who led their forces to victory in 1364, and Andrea del Castagno's related fresco of Niccolò da Tolentino are painted on the interior walls of Florence cathedral, as is a fresco by Domenico di Michelino showing Dante explaining the *Divine Comedy* to the city of Florence (public lectures on Dante were held throughout the fifteenth century as an extension of the university).

More appropriate, to modern eyes at least, are Perugino's allegorical figures of the Virtues and famous men of antiquity that decorate the interior of the exchange office in Perugia—though they are accompanied by depictions of the Nativity and Transfiguration. Ambrogio Lorenzetti's frescoes in the chambers of the rulers of Siena show on one wall an allegory of the origins and virtues of good government and on adjacent walls the effects of good and bad government on city life, depicted with an unprecedented eye to plausibility. In one scene a view of urban life and active trade gives way to a vast, panoramic landscape of southern Tuscany in which crops are harvested and hunters are careful to ride their horses only where the wheat has been cut down, while just visible in the distance is the seaport on which the city placed its vain hopes for maritime trade.

Just as monastic orders used art to spread the faith, so civic governments used the new, more realistic style created by Giotto to propagandize their government. The Sienese captain Guidoriccio da Fogliano presides over one wall of the communal palace in Siena, his conquered, insurgent castle visible in the background, while below him, in a fresco ascribed to Duccio, another town is symbolically handed over to a representative of the Sienese state. These frescoes were calculated to have an intimidating effect on visitors and ambassadors.

The mixture of religion and the state is most apparent in the cult of relics and of local saints which seem to have carried as much prestige for medieval communes as shopping malls do today. In the doge's church of San Marco in Venice, the chief relic was of the apostle Mark, whose remains were brought to the city from Egypt in 829. The greatest Venetian painter of the fourteenth century, Paolo Veneziano, was commissioned to describe the events of the transport for a cover to the gold and enamel Pala d'Oro. In Perugia, the chapel of the Priors' Palace is decorated with fifteenth-century frescoes that show the contemporary rulers of the city participating vicariously in the translation of the relics of Saint Herculanus, the sixth-century bishop of the city, to the cathedral of San Pietro following his death at the hands of Totila. And Ghirlandaio was asked to incorporate portraits of leading civic officials in his depiction of the funeral of Santa Fina in the Collegiata in San Gimignano. The saint's canonization had been promoted by the city, and Ghirlandaio's fresco contains, in the background, the most notable landmarks of San Gimignano, both as a means to historical veracity and as a piece of civic propaganda.

One of the most singular features of city life was the existence of confraternities, which were as much a part of the urban fabric as a police force or fire department today. These organizations performed a host of charitable tasks, ranging from almsgiving to the running of hospitals. They had quarters where members met for prayer and discussion, and each had its own patron saint. It was for one such confraternity in Venice that Gentile Bellini depicted a miracle that took place during the procession of a relic of the holy cross on the Bridge of San Lorenzo in the late fourteenth century. The relic fell into the canal and was only recovered when the guardian of the confraternity, Andrea Vendramin, intervened. The scene reminds us how futile is the modern distinction between religious and secular spheres when it is applied to pre-Reformation society. In the celebrated hospital of Siena, whose foundations go back to the tenth century, the reception room was decorated in the 1440s with frescoes lauding its history and the services it provided, ranging from ministering to the sick, providing bread and clothes for the poor and burial for the dead, to the raising of foundlings.

Duccio (active by 1278, died 1319)
The Maestà, 1308–11
Tempera and gold on wood, 84 x 156" (211.8 x 412.1 cm)
Museo del Opera del Duomo, Siena

Carlo Crivelli (active by 1457, died 1493)
The Annunciation, with Saint Emidius, 1486
Tempera and gold on wood, 81½ x 57¾" (207 x 146.5 cm)
Reproduced by courtesy of the Trustees,
The National Gallery, London

OPPOSITE:
Bernardo Daddi (ca. 1290–after 1355)
Madonna delle Grazie, 1347
Tempera and gold on wood, 98⅜ x 70⅞" (250 x 180 cm)
Orsanmichele, Florence

VOLGETE GLIOCCHI AMIRAR COSTEI VOCHE REGGIETE CHE QVI FIGVRATA Z DISVE ECCELECIA CORONATA LAVNA SEDRA CIASCVN SVO

Ambrogio Lorenzetti (active by 1319, died 1348/49)
Allegory of the Effects of Good Government, 1338–40
Fresco
Sala della Pace, Palazzo Pubblico, Siena

OPPOSITE:
Simone Martini (active by 1315, died 1344)
Guidoriccio da Fogliano, dated 1328
and Duccio (attributed to) (active by 1278, died 1319)
Surrender of a Castle to a Representative of Siena, ca. 1310
Fresco
Palazzo Pubblico, Siena

54

SERVATA · QVESTA · NITV · RDIV' · OLTRA · BISPREOE · ELLA · GVRDE · OIFEOE · CALLA · ODORI · 7 · LOR · INTRICA · 7 · DASCIE · DA · LA · SVO · LVCIE · DASCIE · EL · MERITR · COLOR · COPERA · RENE · 7 · AGLIDIOVI · OR · OERITE · PENE

Piero della Francesca (ca. 1415–1492)
The Resurrection, ca. 1455
Fresco, 88½ x 78¾" (225 x 200 cm)
Pinacoteca, Sansepolcro

Paolo Uccello (1397–1475)
Sir John Hawkwood, 1436
Fresco, transferred to canvas, 322⅞ x 202¾" (820 x 515 cm)
Cathedral, Florence

Domenico di Bartolo (active 1420–1444/45)
Education of the Orphans, 1441–44
Fresco
Pilgrims' Hospice, Hospital of Santa Maria della Scala, Siena

Domenico Ghirlandaio (1449–1494)
Funeral of Santa Fina, ca. 1475
Fresco
Collegiata, San Gimignano

Gentile Bellini (1429–1507)
Miracle of the Cross at the Bridge of San Lorenzo, 1496
Oil on canvas, 144½ x 293⅜" (367 x 745 cm)
Accademia, Venice

7.
Courtly Taste in the Renaissance

Painting for popes and princes from Matteo Giovanetti
to Andrea Mantegna and Giulio Romano

Renaissance art is generally associated with the advent of a powerful, urban middle class with clear-headed, worldly values: the merchants and bankers of fourteenth- and fifteenth-century Florence and Venice. However, those cities that were ruled by a prince, marquis, count, or petty tyrant were numerous, and their impact on the evolution of Italian painting was considerable. Giotto may have been a Florentine by birth, but he worked for both the ruling Visconti family in Milan and King Robert of Anjou in Naples. The Sienese Simone Martini also worked for Robert of Anjou and about 1340 moved to Avignon, where he worked for the papal court (Avignon replaced Rome as the seat of the papacy during 1309–77). The work Simone carried out there became the basis for what has become known as the International Gothic Style, practiced throughout Europe in the second half of the fourteenth century. In the succeeding century, the services of the brilliant engineer, architect, sculptor, and painter Francesco di Giorgio were lent out by the republican government of Siena to Duke Federico da Montefeltro in Urbino, Duke Ludovico Sforza in Milan, and King Ferdinando I in Naples as part of their political alliances. In 1482, Leonardo da Vinci abandoned Medicean Florence for the Sforza court in Milan, where he painted some of his greatest masterpieces (see chapter 10). In these ways, the new artistic style of communal governments gained a foothold in the courts of Italy.

The reverse also happened, though with less frequency. Gentile da Fabriano's success in Florence, where he arrived about 1420, was based on the fame he had acquired while working for the soldier-ruler Pandolfo Malatesta of Brescia in Lombardy. Gentile's gold-encrusted masterpiece, the *Adoration of the Magi*, painted for the richest citizen of Florence, Palla Strozzi, introduced Florentine artists to the refinements of the International Gothic Style popular in north Italian courts. The long-lasting impact of this complex work, which combines remarkable passages of observation with decorative splendor, may be gauged by the fact that Piero de'Medici later hired Benozzo Gozzoli to decorate the interior of his private chapel with frescoes that patently emulate Gentile's altarpiece, thus endowing a private, patrician residence in a putatively republican Florence with a work worthy of a prince. The point was not lost on guests to the palace, who were shown the chapel with justifiable pride.

If the channels of exchange between courts and communes remained open throughout the fourteenth and fifteenth centuries, differences nonetheless pertain. Court patrons could be publicly lavish while private citizens usually found it safer to maintain a certain discreetness. Moreover, until the middle of the fifteenth century, the Este of Ferrara, the Gonzaga of Mantua, the Montefeltro of Urbino, and the Visconti and Sforza of Milan looked to France—not Florence—for cultural guidance, and the works commissioned were conspicuous alike for their chivalric themes and the rich materials used in their execution. That most costly of wall coverings, tapestries, was the decoration of choice; mural painting was frequently a less-expensive alternative. In the early fifteenth century, tapestry workers from northern Europe were established in Mantua and Ferrara, and the court artists of the Gonzaga and the Este—including Andrea Mantegna and Cosimo Tura—occasionally produced cartoons to be translated into wall hangings by foreign weavers. The cycle of murals Ludovico Gonzaga commissioned from Pisanello in the 1440s was in a real sense a substitute for tapestries, and the flat, claustrophobic compositions of the murals, no less than their subject matter (they are based on Arthurian legend), were conditioned by this fact.

The wealthy Borromeo family in Milan, whose fortunes were based on banking, saw to it that, in emulation of the ruler of the city, Francesco Sforza, their residence was decorated with depictions of high-bred men and women indulging in aristocratic games. It was evidently for a member of the Visconti-Sforza family that Bonifacio Bembo and, later, Antonio Cigonara painted their remarkable Tarot cards—a game created expressly for the courts of northern Italy.

Although French culture reigned supreme at Italian courts in the fourteenth and early fifteenth centuries, this did not inhibit the Este and the Gonzaga from hiring humanists to teach their children Greek and Latin and instruct them in the literature of ancient Rome. Lionello d'Este of Ferrara was a patron of Pisanello, Jacopo Bellini, Rogier van der Weyden, and Andrea Mantegna, as well as a friend of that remarkable humanist writer, theorist, architect, and mathematician, Leon Battista Alberti. Under Lionello's reign and that of his brother Borso a new, indigenous style emerged that combined the elegant complexities of Gothic art with the most modern innovations of the Renaissance. For a private study in the Este retreat at Belfiore Cosimo Tura painted a figure of a classical muse who has the surreal, rarefied appearance of a hybrid orchid, her self-conscious gesture reminiscent of a ballerina (Ferrara was, in fact, a center of music and dance). No less remarkable are the frescoes painted by Francesco del Cossa in Borso d'Este's pleasure-palace, the Palazzo Schifanoia (meaning "flee boredom"). Is it any wonder that it was for the Este court that the poet Matteo Maria Boiardo laid the foundation of Renaissance epic poetry, with its amalgam of chivalric and classical literary traditions?

If, in Mantua, court art evolved into something more authentically classical, this was because Ludovico Gonzaga managed to procure the services of Andrea Mantegna, who in 1460 moved from the university town of Padua to Mantua, where he served three generations of Gonzaga rulers. Mantegna had a more profound knowledge of classical antiquity than any other painter, and through his work, members of the Gonzaga court came to visualize themselves as the heirs of imperial Rome (the Roman poet Vergil had been a Mantuan). The dramatic shift in taste in Mantua after Mantegna's arrival is readily illustrated by comparing the French-inspired cycle of murals Ludovico Gonzaga commissioned from Pisanello in the 1440s was in a real sense a substitute for tapestries, and the flat, claustrophobic compositions of the murals, no less than their subject matter (they are based on Arthurian legend), were conditioned by this fact.

Just as, in the early fifteenth century, the courts had served as a conduit for French culture in Italy, they played a major role in introducing classical Renaissance culture to France and the rest of Europe. Mantegna's successor at Mantua, Giulio Romano—an incomparable racconteur of classical myths—became the most famous artist of his day, and his assistant Primaticcio was brought to France by Francis I to superintend the decoration of that outstanding monument of French Renaissance culture, the chateau of Fontainebleau.

Anonymous Lombard (active 6th decade of the 15th century)
Women Playing Cards, 1450s
Fresco
Palazzo Borromeo, Milan

Matteo Giovanetti
(ca. 1300–1368/69)
Scene of Fishing, 1346–48
Fresco
Pope's Palace, Avignon

Anonymous Piemontese
(active 2nd quarter of
15th century)
Fountain of Youth, ca. 1430–50
Fresco
Castle of La Manta, Cúneo

OPPOSITE:
Anonymous North Italian
Cycle of the Months (May),
shortly before 1407
Fresco
Torre Aquila, Castel
del Buonconsiglio, Trent

Bonifacio Bembo (active between 1444 and 1477)
Playing Cards (The Chariot, The Fool), ca. 1450–60
Tempera, gold, and silver on cardboard, 7 x 3½" (17.6 x 8.7 cm)
The Pierpont Morgan Library, New York

Francesco del Cossa (ca. 1435–ca. 1477)
The Court of Borso d'Este under the Sign of Venus, ca. 1470
Fresco
Palazzo Schifanoia, Ferrara

OPPOSITE:
Andrea Mantegna (ca. 1430–1506)
Camera Picta (Meeting of Ludovico and Francesco Gonzaga), 1470–74
Fresco
Palazzo Ducale, Mantua

Andrea Mantegna (ca. 1430–1506)
The Triumphs of Caesar (canvas II: *Colossal Statues on Carts*), 1482–92
Distemper on canvas, 89 x 109½" (226 x 278 cm)
Royal Collection, St. James's Palace, London

OVERLEAF:
Giulio Romano (1499–1546)
Marriage of Cupid and Psyche, 1527–28
Fresco
Palazzo Te, Mantua

ET·REIP·FLOR· CAPIT

8.
The Primacy of Drawing in Tuscan Painting

Florentine painting from Cimabue to Cigoli

From the late thirteenth century until the middle of the sixteenth, the tone of Italian painting was set by artists born in or near Florence. It was Giotto who, in the words of a later follower, Cennino Cennini, had "changed the profession of painting from Greek"—what we would call the Byzantine style—"back into Latin, and brought it up to date." It was Masaccio who probed the fallible character of humanity and its struggle in a sometimes hostile environment. And it was Michelangelo who endowed humankind with a godlike beauty and noble, transcendent soul.

The focus of Florentine painting was man. Nature invariably played a supporting rather than a primary role, and the preferred means of description was the pen or other drawing instrument. "It is not without the impulse of a lofty spirit that some are moved to enter this profession," wrote Cennino in his handbook on painting, which dates from the late fourteenth or early fifteenth century. "Their intellect will take delight in drawing, provided their nature attracts them to it of themselves, without any master's guidance, out of loftiness of spirit." It was told that Giotto, the father of Florentine painting, was discovered by Cimabue in the countryside, drawing the sheep he was tending onto a flat stone. A second story, recounted by the sixteenth-century painter and biographer Giorgio Vasari, relates that as an example of his work Giotto sent Pope Benedict XI a sheet of paper on which he had drawn, without mechanical aids, a perfect circle. In this work the pope immediately recognized the artist's genius, not simply because of the facility required to make a perfect circle freehand, but because the drawing had an implied conceit, the Italian word for circle, *tondo,* meaning also a slow-witted simpleton.

As these anecdotes demonstrate, drawing was associated with the mind and with that much prized Florentine attribute, wit, and it had already acquired a preeminent status in the time of Giotto. To the followers of Michelangelo, drawing, or *disegno,* meant not merely the act of describing a figure or an object placed before the artist, but the process whereby ordinary matter was transformed by the intellect into a paradigm of beauty: an act combining skill, knowledge, and inspiration. In such a conception, color assumed an ornamental character. It was either used functionally, to reinforce or sustain the overall design of a picture, or to embellish the work. In the large altarpieces by Cimabue and Giotto showing the Madonna and Child enthroned with angels, bright, contrasting colors are distributed symmetrically to build up the composition in a logical, coherent fashion. Not even a painter from Siena, the other major Tuscan city, south of Florence, would have reduced color to such a subsidiary role. In Lorenzo Monaco's *Coronation of the Virgin,* painted in 1414, and Pontormo's *Entombment,* painted about 1526–28, color is exploited for its intrinsic, decorative properties, divorced from any mimetic effect. "This combining of colors will enhance the attractiveness of the painting by its variety, and its beauty by its comparisons," wrote

Leon Battista Alberti in his treatise on painting, composed in 1435. "There is a kind of sympathy among colors, whereby their grace and beauty is increased when they are placed side by side."

Grace and beauty—*grazia* and *bellezza*—are crucial terms in Florentine criticism. They refer not merely to demeanor and comportment—the way a figure stands or performs even a simple or menial task with composure and elegance—but the quality of character and mind these external features were believed to reflect. By extension, ugliness was the expression of a mean spirit. There is no such thing as a casual or unpremeditated action in Florentine painting.

The invention of perspective and the study of anatomy, which first come together in the work of Masaccio, gave Florentine painting an intellectual edge which artists were loath to abandon. Late in life, Piero della Francesca, who was a Florentine by training rather than by birth, devoted much of his time to writing a treatise on perspective, firm in the belief that those who did not appreciate it "have no knowledge of the possibility of art." He had been preceded in this obsession by Paolo Uccello.

Antonio del Pollaiuolo devoted equal enthusiasm to the study of anatomy. His *Saint Sebastian* might be criticized for the degree to which the religious subject has been seized as an opportunity to demonstrate the artist's unprecedented mastery of the human figure and his newfound use of mannequins to study complicated poses: we recognize that the six executioners are evolved from just two models that have been rotated to obtain the various poses. In Leonardo da Vinci's hands, painting became an instrument for investigating and describing the world: it is impossible to fully appreciate his imaginative landscapes or the shadows that envelope his figures—those effects of *sfumato*—without recourse to his voluminous notes on the origins of mountains and the properties of light. Yet, for all their obsession with observation and analysis, these two artists were never content to merely describe Nature. They sought to abstract from it what they saw as universal laws or principles. Leonardo's infatuation with what had begun as a portrait of a Florentine beauty, Lisa del Giocondo (the picture we know as the *Gioconda* or the *Mona Lisa:* Milady Lisa), had to do with the convergence of an actual person's appearance with the artist's own ideas about *grazia* and *bellezza*.

Sharpness of mind is a curious thing. It dislikes ambiguity but is tolerant of eccentricity; spurns the accidental but prizes the imaginative; is quick to condemn mediocrity but can fall prey to academicism and mere cleverness. Florentine art exhibits all of these tendencies. It was the product of clearheadedness and critical faculties sharpened by the experience of external events. The economic failures and Black Death of the mid-fourteenth century inform the stern, apocalyptic vision of Orcagna's great altarpiece of Christ giving the keys of heaven to Saint Peter, commissioned in 1354 and completed in 1357. In the late fifteenth century the inflammatory sermons and religious reform of the Ferrarese Dominican monk Savonarola led Botticelli to sacrifice the sensual beauties of his earlier work for a sinewy, even uningratiating style exemplificative of a state of moral purity. The replacement of Florentine republicanism by the princely power of the Medici found its finest response in the mid-sixteenth-century portraits of Bronzino, who managed to glorify without fawning and to describe the features of his sitters faithfully without ever appearing banal. At the end of the sixteenth century, a friend of Gallileo, Cigoli, knew how to salvage the finest of his Florentine heritage and wed it to a renewed study of nature through the coloristic splendor of Titian, thereby laying the groundwork for a native baroque style.

Cimabue (active 1272–1302)
Madonna of Santa Trinità, ca. 1280
Tempera and gold on wood, 151½ x 87¾" (385 x 223 cm)
Galleria degli Uffizi, Florence

Giotto (1266–1337)
The Ognissanti Madonna, ca. 1305–10
Tempera and gold on wood, 128 x 80⅜" (325 x 204 cm)
Galleria degli Uffizi, Florence

Maso di Banco (active 1336–1346)
Saint Silvester Closes the Mouth of a Dragon and Resuscitates Two Magi, ca. 1336
Fresco
Santa Croce, Florence

Pietro Lorenzetti (active by 1306, died after 1344)
The Birth of the Virgin, 1342
Tempera and gold on wood, 73⅝ x 71⅝" (187 x 182 cm)
Museo del Duomo, Siena

Andrea Orcagna (active ca. 1343, died 1368/69)
Christ Giving the Keys to Saint Peter, with Saints, dated 1357
Tempera and gold on wood, 63 x 116½" (160 x 296 cm)
Strozzi Chapel, Santa Maria Novella, Florence

Lorenzo Monaco (before 1372, died after 1422)
Coronation of the Virgin, 1414
Tempera and gold on wood, 177⅛ x 137¾" (450 x 350 cm)
Galleria degli Uffizi, Florence

Masolino (1383–1440)
The Fall of Man, ca. 1425
Fresco, 81⅞ x 34⅝" (208 x 88 cm)
Brancacci Chapel, Santa Maria del Carmine, Florence

Masaccio (1401–1428)
Expulsion of Adam and Eve, ca. 1425
Fresco, 81⅞ x 34⅝" (208 x 88 cm)
Brancacci Chapel, Santa Maria del Carmine, Florence

Domenico Veneziano (active by 1438, died 1461)
Saint Lucy Altarpiece, ca. 1445–50
Tempera on wood, 82¼ x 85" (209 x 216 cm)
Galleria degli Uffizi, Florence

Filippo Lippi (1406–1469)
The Annunciation, ca. 1440
Tempera on wood, 68⅛ x 72" (175 x 183 cm)
San Lorenzo, Florence

Filippino Lippi (1457–1504)
The Vision of Saint Bernard, ca. 1485
Oil on wood, 82⅝ x 76¾" (210 x 195 cm)
Badia, Florence

Piero della Francesca (ca. 1415–1492)
Baptism of Christ, ca. 1450
Tempera on wood, 66 x 45¾" (167 x 116 cm)
Reproduced by courtesy of the Trustees,
The National Gallery, London

OPPOSITE:
Verrocchio (ca. 1435–1488) assisted by
Leonardo da Vinci (1452–1519)
Baptism of Christ, ca. 1475
Tempera and oil on wood, 69⅝ x 59½" (177 x 151 cm)
Galleria degli Uffizi, Florence

84

85

Andrea del Castagno (1417/19–1457)
The Youthful David Slaying Goliath, ca. 1450
Tempera on leather mounted on wood
45½ x 30¼" (115.6 x 76.9 cm)
National Gallery of Art, Washington
Widener Collection

Sandro Botticelli (1445–1510)
Madonna and Child with Angels, ca. 1477
Tempera and gold on wood
diameter 53⅛" (135 cm)
Gemäldegalerie, Staatliche Museen, Berlin

Michelangelo (1475–1564)
The Holy Family (Doni Tondo), shown in its original frame, 1503–4
Tempera on wood, diameter 47½" (120 cm)
Galleria degli Uffizi, Florence

ECCE AGNIVS
DEI

OPPOSITE:
Luca Signorelli
(ca. 1441–1523)
The Holy Family, ca. 1490
Oil on wood, 67 x 46½"
(170 x 117.5 cm)
Galleria degli Uffizi,
Florence

Leonardo da Vinci
(1452–1519)
*The Madonna and Child
with Saint John the Baptist
and an Angel*, called
The Virgin of the Rocks,
1483–86 (?)
Oil on wood, 78¾ x 48⅛"
(199 x 122 cm)
Musée du Louvre, Paris

91

Fra Bartolommeo (1472–1517)
*God the Father Adored by Saint Catherine of Siena
and the Magdalen*, 1509
Oil on canvas, 142 x 93" (361 x 236 cm)
Pinacoteca Nazionale
di Villa Guinigi, Lucca

OPPOSITE:
Rosso Fiorentino (1496–1540)
The Dead Christ with Angels, ca. 1525
Oil on wood, 52½ x 41" (133.5 x 104.1 cm)
Museum of Fine Arts, Boston
Charles Potter Kling Fund

Pontormo (1494–1557)
Entombment, ca. 1526–28
Oil on wood, 123¼ x 75½" (313 x 192 cm)
Santa Felicita, Florence

Domenico Beccafumi (1486–1551)
Descent into Limbo, ca. 1536
Oil on wood, 155½ x 88⅝" (395 x 225 cm)
Pinacoteca Nazionale, Siena

OPPOSITE:
Ludovico Cigoli (1559–1613)
Saint Jerome in His Study, 1599
Oil on wood, 162½ x 81⅛" (412 x 206 cm)
San Giovanni dei Fiorentini, Rome

9.
The Color of Venice

Painting in the Serenissima from Paolo Veneziano to Tiepolo

The great sixteenth-century Venetian painter Tintoretto is reported to have had written on the walls of his studio "the drawing of Michelangelo and the color of Titian." Shallow though such an adage may sound, it nonetheless characterizes Tintoretto's ambition not simply to emulate the greatest masters of the preceding generation, but to bring together what had been seen as the two irreconcilable poles of Italian painting. For it is no exaggeration to state that in the work of Titian and Michelangelo, sixteenth-century artists and critics saw two diametrically opposed approaches to painting, the one emphasizing an art based on optical perceptions of the world around us—an art of sensual experience; the other seeing in art a cognitive process by which the imperfections of what we would call the "real world" acquired an ideal beauty and perfection. Titian and Michelangelo knew each other's work, and Titian was certainly influenced by the example of the great Florentine. During a visit to Rome in 1545–46, he painted a canvas showing Danae receiving the love of Jupiter in a shower of gold coins (Museo Nazionale di Capodimonte, Naples) as a response to Michelangelo's vaunted mastery of the nude (typically, the Venetian chose a female rather than a male nude as his subject). The picture was greatly admired by Michelangelo for its color, but he added that it was a shame Venetian artists did not begin their training by learning to draw. It was this gulf that Tintoretto sought to bridge, and in a picture like his *Saint Mark Liberating the Slave*, with its audacious foreshortenings and mastery of the human figure—the special province of Michelangelo and Florentine painting—conveyed with the coloristic brilliance and tonal unity of a work by Titian, he seems actually to achieve this seemingly impossible goal.

Where did the Venetian emphasis on color originate? The answer usually offered is that it is part of the physical experience of Venice, with her hazy light and polychromed buildings. Or that the tendency derives from the practice of working in mosaics, in which individually colored tesserae are artfully arranged to create an optically coherent image. The problem is that mosaics were made in Florence as well as Venice and seem to have had little if any effect on the practice of painting. Indeed, in the early fifteenth century, Florentine artists had to be imported to Venice to carry out mosaics in the Basilica of San Marco, since the craft had fallen into decline since the halcyon days of the thirteenth century. If the peculiar taste of Venetian artists for rich, sumptuous colors has a specific source, it is in the trade routes that linked the city with the Middle East.

It is a well-known fact that all Italians—Venetians and Florentines alike—prized the brocaded fabrics and carpets imported from the Middle East and that these textiles found their way into their paintings, but nowhere was the trade as intense and longstanding as in Venice. The delicately patterned damask in which the fourteenth-century painter Paolo Veneziano clothed his saints and Madonnas found no equivalent in the work of Giotto. Venice was also at the center of the trade in pigments, especially of lapis lazuli blue, or ultramarine (the name refers to the fact that it was shipped from abroad). Oriental splendor remained a constant of Venetian fashion, whether in dress or the Turkish-inspired stamping on sixteenth-century book bindings.

There was another, historical factor that contributed to the differences between Venetian art and that of the mainland: the city's centuries-old ties with the Byzantine Empire and the constant contact with Greek artists, which persisted down to the arrival in Venice of El Greco in the sixteenth century. For all of the transformations Byzantine art had undergone since Constantinople had become the capital of the eastern Roman Empire, it still preserved in stylized form a late-antique, impressionistic approach to color and light. This was consciously revived by Paolo Veneziano in the fourteenth century and became the basis for the achievements of Venetian colorism at the hands of Giovanni Bellini, Giorgione, and Titian in the fifteenth and sixteenth centuries.

Venetian art tended to move ahead through contact with outside stimuli. In the early fifteenth century, the Marchigian painter Gentile da Fabriano was employed by the Venetian state, and his pupil there, Jacopo Bellini, seems to have gone with him to Florence. The Florentines Andrea del Castagno and Paolo Uccello worked in Venice while Filippo Lippi and Donatello were active in nearby Padua. Jacopo Bellini and Antonio Vivarini first introduced some of the novelties of Florentine painting into Venice—especially a concern for perspective. In 1453, Andrea Mantegna, whose art had been formed in the shadow of Donatello, married Jacopo Bellini's daughter. Mantegna's art provided the model for Jacopo's talented son, Giovanni Bellini, who in turn laid the basis for Venetian Renaissance painting. According to Vasari, Leonardo da Vinci's short visit to Venice in 1500 inspired Giorgione's approach to atmospheric painting, and Titian struck up a close friendship with the transplanted Florentine sculptor Jacopo Sansovino.

The process was renewed in the seventeenth century by the arrival in Venice of Domenico Fetti, who had been trained in Rome by the Florentine Ludovico Cigoli and who was greatly influenced by Rubens. He brought with him a painterly style that accorded with Venetian ideas about brushwork and color, and this style established the basis for Venetian baroque painting.

The reverse process was, however, of far greater consequence. Titian's paintings were avidly collected throughout Europe, from Prague to Madrid, and their impact on Flemish and Spanish art is incalculable. The work of Rubens, Velázquez, and Rembrandt would be inconceivable without the prior study of the paintings of Titian and his use of color to achieve greater immediacy and sensual vividness.

Despite the efforts of Tintoretto, Venetian and Florentine art remained separate, and the tug-of-war between Florentine drawing and Venetian color—of a cerebral versus a sensual approach to art—became an animating factor in European painting, resurfacing in a variety of guises, pitting the supporters of Poussin against those of Rubens; Ingres against Delacroix; and Picasso against Matisse.

OPPOSITE:
Paolo Veneziano (active by 1333, died 1358/62)
Coronation of the Virgin, ca. 1350
Tempera and gold on wood, 38½ x 24¾" (98 x 63 cm)
Accademia, Venice

Antonello da Messina (active by 1456, died 1479)
Saint Jerome in His Study, ca. 1475
Oil on wood, 18 x 14¼" (46 x 36.5 cm)
Reproduced by courtesy of the Trustees,
The National Gallery, London

Giorgione (1476/77–1510)
Three Philosophers, ca. 1508–10
Oil on canvas, 48¾ x 56⅞" (123.8 x 144.5 cm)
Kunsthistorisches Museum, Vienna

Cima da Conegliano (1459/60–1517/18)
Saint John the Baptist and Four Saints, 1493–95
Oil on wood, 120 x 80¾" (305 x 205 cm)
Chiesa della Madonna dell'Orto, Venice

Pordenone (148⅜4–1539)
Blessed Lorenzo Giustiniani Altarpiece, 1532
Oil on canvas, 165½ x 86⅝" (420 x 220 cm)
Accademia, Venice

OPPOSITE TOP:
Jacopo Bassano (1517–1592)
The Flight into Egypt, ca. 1544–45
Oil on canvas, 48½ x 77¼" (123.2 x 196.2 cm)
Norton Simon Art Foundation

Jacopo Tintoretto (1514–1594)
Saint Mark Liberating the Slave, 1547–48
Oil on canvas, 163½ x 213⅛" (415 x 541 cm)
Accademia, Venice

OPPOSITE BOTTOM:
Lorenzo Lotto (ca. 1480–1556)
Holy Family with Saint Catherine, ca. 1529
Oil on canvas, 44½ x 59⅞" (113 x 152 cm)
Kunsthistorisches Museum, Vienna

OPPOSITE:
Paolo Veronese (1528–1588)
The Mystic Marriage of Saint Catherine, ca. 1575
Oil on canvas, 132⅝ x 94⅞" (337 x 241 cm)
Accademia, Venice

Giovanni Battista Piazzetta (1683–1754)
Custodian Angel, ca. 1740
Oil on canvas, 98⅜ x 44" (250 x 112 cm)
Church of San Vitale, Venice

Giambattista Tiepolo (1696–1770)
Madonna and Child with Saints Catherine,
Rosa, and Agnes, ca. 1740
Oil on canvas, 133⅞ x 66⅛" (340 x 168 cm)
Church of the Gesuati, Venice

10.
Painters of Reality

Painting in and around Lombardy in the 14ᵗʰ–18ᵗʰ centuries

To most of us today, Italian painting of the fifteenth and sixteenth centuries is confined to Venice and Florence, while in the seventeenth century attention shifts to Rome. However, the geography and political subdivisions of Italy were far more complex than this schematic view suggests. From the fourteenth through the eighteenth century, the area in and around Milan—Lombardy—was home to a series of outstanding artists whose work may have been touched by that of Florence to the south and Venice to the east, but remained nonetheless distinct. The same is true of painting in Bologna and the numerous smaller cities and courts in the surrounding plain, south of the Po river. In the early seventeenth century the Bolognese prelate and critic Giovanni Battista Agucchi discerned four major schools of painting: those of Florence, Venice, Rome, and Lombardy.

Northern Italian painting has never enjoyed a prominent treatment in surveys of Italian art, which is ironical considering that in the seventeenth century it all but usurped the position formerly held by Florentine and Venetian painting. The matter is made graphically clear in Giovanni Pietro Bellori's influential *Lives of Modern Painters, Sculptors and Architects,* published in 1672. Bellori had no difficulty in identifying the origins of Italian painting in Cimabue and Giotto in Florence and its climax in the work of Raphael in Rome. However, from that point the graph seemed to him one of decline, artifice and mannerism triumphing over the study of nature. This state of affairs was transformed by two artists who arrived in Rome from northern Italy in the 1590s. Their names were Caravaggio and Annibale Carracci, and although to their contemporaries they would both have been considered Lombard artists, their methods and the traditions which formed their work were so different that it is best to let the Po River have its way and treat the regions from which they came—to the north and south—in separate chapters.

Upon his arrival in Rome in 1593, Caravaggio, who was trained in Milan, was pigeonholed as a typical Lombard artist: someone, that is, totally given over to painting directly from nature, with little or no concern for the higher spheres to which Art might aspire. In the early sixteenth century another northern Italian painter, Giovanni da Udine, had been employed in Raphael's workshop painting the border decorations of fruits and foliage on the vault of the Villa Farnesina and the still life of musical instruments in Raphael's altarpiece of Saint Cecilia. So we should not be surprised that, according to early biographers, Caravaggio was employed in a similar capacity by the leading Roman painter, the Cavalier d'Arpino. Among Caravaggio's earliest works were genre and still-life paintings, and only gradually did he manage to secure a position as a figure painter. Curious though this may seem to us, it was inevitable, for in the late sixteenth century naturalism was seen as the hallmark of Lombard art.

It is not easy to pinpoint when the notion of Lombard artists as painters of reality originated, but it is certainly true that by the sixteenth century naturalism was commonly held to be as synonymous with Lombard painting as drawing was to Florentine and color to Venetian. Titian recommended to Venetian governors of the city of Bergamo that they have their likenesses painted by Giovanni Battista Moroni, "who would do them naturalistically." And Vasari praised the work of Moroni's teacher, Moretto da Brescia, for the manner in which he painted richly patterned drapery and naturalistic heads. These compliments were equivocal in that they implied that Lombard painting was, to a degree, artless.

Whether it is legitimate to trace this tradition of naturalism back to the fourteenth century and the work of Giovanni da Milano, who worked in Florence as well as in and around Milan, is not clear, but it is true that Giovanni's art already showed a concern for carefully described physiognomic details and an attention to still-life elements uncommon at that date. Some of these same traits reappear in the early fifteenth century in the miniatures and very rare panel paintings of Michelino da Besozzo, one of the most famous painters of his day. Michelino was keenly attuned to French courtly traditions and the elegantly artificial style they entailed, but he was also a marvelous observer of flora and fauna, which he drew into notebooks that were copied and passed around admiringly. In the second half of the fifteenth century, Vincenzo Foppa took up the thread, creating devotional pictures of the Madonna and Child at once homely, intimate, and refined. Paradoxically, the artist who turned this latent tradition into an articulated artistic position was Leonardo da Vinci, who abandoned his native Florence for Milan in 1482. He worked in the Lombard capital until 1499 and then again between 1506 and 1513, painting some of his most familiar masterpieces there. His mural of the *Last Supper,* carried out in an unsuccessful, experimental technique, was already a ruin in the mid-sixteenth century and today is little more than a shadow best appreciated in old copies and engravings. Nonetheless, a painstaking recent cleaning has salvaged still-life details of astonishing beauty: a slice of an orange reflected in a silver dish; the woven pattern of the blue embroidered tablecloth; and swags of ripe fruit decorating the lunettes above the main scene. Similar features are found in Moretto da Brescia's noble *Christ in the House of the Pharisee* and in Caravaggio's *Supper at Emmaus* (National Gallery, London), and they are the basis of the earliest Lombard still-life paintings of the late sixteenth century (see chapter 24). To judge from Leonardo's contemporary altarpiece in the Louvre, the *Virgin of the Rocks,* this remarkable descriptive ability must have characterized the figures of the apostles in the *Last Supper,* and it goes a long way to explaining the astonishing *Christ at the Column* painted by Leonardo's great contemporary Bramante, better known today as an architect. Leonardo's interest in atmospheric effects and in capturing fleeting expressions (what he referred to as the movements of the mind) was passed on to his followers and is the subject of numerous notes in his copious writings. These ideas were still vital to Caravaggio's artistic formation in Milan in the 1580s.

Defining naturalism is not a simple task, for our perception of the world is bound up with assumptions and expectations that fluctuate according to time and place. For Leonardo, nature was a mysteriously generative force, and his pictures are compelling statements of ambiguity. For Bramantino, who belonged to a younger generation and was a passionate devotee of perspective, the key to nature was more strongly rooted in mathematics (though he was keenly aware of the atmospheric beauties of Leonardo's art). For the Brescian Girolamo Savoldo, who spent much of his career in Venice, painting was a more straightforward process of description, and his landscape backgrounds are among the first to suggest the real rather than imagined beauty of northern Italy. Gaudenzio Ferrari in the sixteenth century and Cerano, Procaccini, and Morazzone in the seventeenth were less interested in recording the appearance of the world around them than in exploring a means of capturing those animating forces that impart life and movement. Their sometimes extravagantly balletic pictures may seem a far cry from the hyper-subtle poetry of Leonardo, but they were nonetheless indebted to his ideas about beauty and movement.

What Leonardo was to sixteenth-century Lombard painting, Caravaggio was to the seventeenth, establishing what amounted to a manifesto of naturalism. Caravaggio's art determined the character of still-life painting for the entire century. Not surprisingly, the great genre painter of the eighteenth century, Giacomo Ceruti, was a Lombard, and in the nineteenth century Pellizza da Volpedo drew upon a then centuries-old tradition of naturalism to give revolutionary force to his politically charged *The Fourth Estate* (see chapter 26).

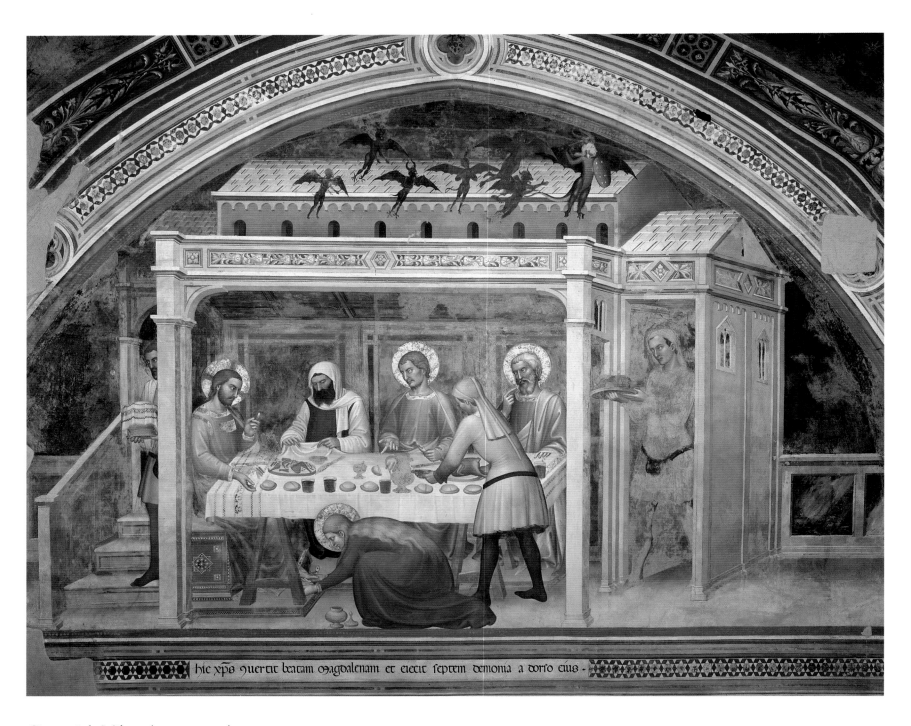

hic xps quertt beatam magdalenam et eiecit septem demonia a dorso eius ·

Giovanni da Milano (ca. 1320–1369)
Christ in the House of the Pharisee, 1365
Fresco
Rinuccini Chapel, Sacristy of
Santa Croce, Florence

OPPOSITE:
Vincenzo Foppa (1427/30–1515/16)
Madonna and Child, ca. 1480
Oil on wood, 24 x 15" (61 x 38 cm)
Museo Poldi Pezzoli, Milan

113

Bramante (1444–1514)
Christ at the Column, ca. 1480–81
Oil on wood, 36⅝ x 24⅜" (93 x 62 cm)
Pinacoteca di Brera, Milan

OPPOSITE:
Bramantino (ca. 1465–1530)
The Crucifixion, ca. 1510–11
Oil on canvas, 146½ x 106¼" (372 x 270 cm)
Pinacoteca di Brera, Milan

115

Andrea Solario (1470/74–1514)
Annunciation, 1506
Oil on wood, 30 x 30¾" (76 x 78 cm)
Musée du Louvre, Paris

OPPOSITE:
Girolamo Romanino (1484/87–1559/61)
Saint Matthew and the Angel, 1520–24
Oil on canvas, 80¾ x 38⅝" (205 x 98 cm)
Chapel of the Sacrament, San Giovanni
Evangelista, Brescia

117

Giovanni Girolamo Savoldo (active 1508–1548)
Shepherd with a Flute, ca. 1525
Oil on canvas, 38⅝₆ x 30¹¹₁₆" (97 x 78 cm)
The J. Paul Getty Museum, Malibu, California

Moretto da Brescia (ca. 1498–1554)
Christ in the House of the Pharisee, ca. 1550–54
Oil on canvas, 81½ x 55⅛" (207 x 140 cm)
Santa Maria in Calchera, Brescia

Cerano (1575/76–1632),
Giulio Cesare Procaccini (1551–1629),
and Morazone (1573–1616)
Martyrdom of Saints Ruffina and Seconda
(The Altarpiece of Three Hands), ca. 1622–25
Oil on canvas, 75⅝ x 75⅝" (192 x 192 cm)
Pinacoteca di Brera, Milan

Caravaggio (1571–1610)
Rest on the Flight into Egypt, ca. 1596–97
Oil on canvas, 53⅜ x 65½" (135.5 x 166.5 cm)
Galleria Doria Pamphili, Rome

II.
Art and Nature

Painting in Emilia Romagna and the Marches in the 14ᵗʰ–18ᵗʰ centuries

An artist's reputation has always depended on public exposure and the accolades of a cross section of critics. In the days before art galleries and museums, churches were the most likely setting for this exposure, and an altarpiece or fresco cycle in a chapel was the most probable vehicle. Time and again we read accounts of the impact one or another altarpiece made and the discussions among connoisseurs and worshipers it inspired. One such account concerns an altarpiece painted by Annibale Carracci for the church of San Nicolò in Bologna in 1583. Its subject was conventional: the crucified Christ with figures of the Virgin Mary and saints (including Saint Petronius, patron of Bologna, shown with a model of the city at his feet). However, the style of the altarpiece—the figure of Christ shown head on with unidealized features and the Virgin and saints with the physiognomy of ordinary people—ran counter to prevailing norms. To many critics it seemed as if Annibale had forgotten who it was he was supposed to portray. They found the naturalism of the work and the broad, almost coarse brushwork unsuitable or indecorous. It was one thing to use posed models for studies leading up to a finished work, but quite another to introduce them in this direct fashion into an altarpiece intended for an ecclesiastical setting: "The Good and the Beautiful in art consist not in working up a composition piecemeal from models, but in profiting from experience and in obtaining a resolution in the picture of the fruits of past labors and a well-stocked, disciplined memory."

According to Annibale's primary local biographer, so strong was the criticism that Annibale and his brother Agostino met with their older cousin Ludovico Carracci to discuss what course they ought to take. The three Carracci had spearheaded an artistic reform based on a return to nature and life studies. Had they, perhaps, erred in taking this reform into the precincts of the Church? How might they bring their work more into line with ecclesiastical requirements of decorum without sacrificing the mainspring of their reform? The answer came almost immediately and is exemplified in such mature works as Ludovico Carracci's *Madonna degli Scalzi* and Annibale Carracci's *San Ludovico Altar*, both painted toward the end of the 1580s. Without abandoning those effects of immediacy arrived at by studying models posed in the studio and the implementation of a loose (though no longer heavy or broken) brushwork that aimed at describing an active, animating light, they yet ennobled their figures and beautified their settings on the example of such earlier northern Italian painters as Parmigianino (in the case of Ludovico), Correggio (in the case of Annibale), as well as Veronese. The result was a conscious synthesis of Art and Nature that became the basis of baroque painting throughout Europe. (During his youthful stay in Italy, Rubens copied Annibale's later work in Rome and studied Ludovico's in Bologna and Mantua, where he served the Gonzaga court.)

The generation of Bolognese artists who preceded the Carracci had, for the most part, practiced a style based on Florentine art. Some had actually worked in Florence with Giorgio Vasari, and their pictures were conspicuous for their artificiality: self-consciously artful poses and a paint surface worked up to a hard, enamel-like brilliance that emphasized the drawn contours at the expense of an effect of naturalness. The Carracci owned their own copy of Vasari's famous *Lives*, which they seem to have committed to memory, despite the fact that they took exception to almost every Florentine-biased artistic tenet he put forward. In the margins they penned their sometimes vitriolic comments, such as: "Signor Vasari doesn't realize that the good ancient masters based their work on life. Rather, he would have it that the good artist bases his work on nature secondhand in the works of classical antiquity instead of on the primary and principal source, which is nature herself, which ought always to be imitated. But Vasari knows nothing about art." The comment demonstrates that the Carracci were not slouches when it came to having read their sources on the famous Greek and Roman painters, but they refused to make ancient works of art their primary source of style. What they proposed as an alternative to Florentine mannerist conventions, with their emphasis on facility and artfulness, was a northern Italian mode emphasizing the study of nature. "The Lombard style will prevail," Annibale is said to have exclaimed. In opposition to Michelangelo, they affirmed the example of Correggio, who had been active in Parma, to the north of Bologna; and in opposition to Raphael, they put forward Parmigianino.

Correggio remains a surprisingly under-appreciated master, considering that his influence on Western art has been almost as significant as that of his contemporaries Raphael, Michelangelo, Titian, and Leonardo. It was Correggio's vision of an approachable humanity, ennobled by a feminine feeling for beauty, his emphasis on a delicately modulated emotionalism, and his use of magical light effects to animate his rhapsodic compositions that became the reference point both of seventeenth-century baroque and eighteenth-century rococo artists. And it was through the study of Correggio's paintings that Federico Barocci—together with Veronese and Tintoretto the outstanding painter of the second half of the sixteenth century—was able to create those works that were to serve as beacons for the generation of the Carracci. Barocci lived out his life in the isolated duchy of Urbino, but the altarpieces he sent to Rome caused a sensation, and his *Madonna del Popolo*, painted for the Tuscan city of Arezzo in place of a work commissioned earlier from Vasari, redirected the course of Florentine painting through the admiration it aroused in Cigoli (see chapter 8). It was through Barocci's example that the Carracci rediscovered Correggio.

By the time the Carracci appeared on the scene, Bologna already had behind it a centuries-old heritage as a cultural center, but it was the prominence Bolognese painting acquired through the Carracci's widespread influence that led local historians to rescue from oblivion so remarkable an artist as Vitale da Bologna, who was active in the fourteenth century. His captivating pictures present perhaps the most cogent case for an indigenous, popular-based style that evolved in direct response to the more elevated language of Giotto. (Recent scholarship has been able to establish the outlines of Vitale's gifted predecessors, all of whom, however, remain anonymous.) In the late fifteenth century, under the rule of the Bentivoglio family, Bologna had a second golden age, hosting artists such as Francesco del Cossa, Ercole de'Roberti, and Lorenzo Costa from nearby Ferrara, and spawning such local talent as Francesco Francia. However, the period in which Bolognese painting acquired a renown equal to that of the city's university—the oldest and among the most illustrious in Europe—is unquestionably the seventeenth century: the age of the Carracci, of Guido Reni, and of Guercino (who was from Cento, midway between Ferrara and Bologna). Each of these artists, their contemporaries, and their remarkable successors—perhaps most notably Giuseppe Maria Crespi (see chapter 25)—followed the course the Carracci had charted, with its emphasis on a study of nature and a strong sense of regional identity.

Vitale da Bologna (ca. 1309–before 1361)
The Adoration of the Magi, ca. 1350
Tempera and gold on wood
22¾ x 15¼" (60.4 x 39 cm)
National Gallery of Scotland, Edinburgh

Correggio (ca. 1489–1534)
The Adoration of the Shepherds (The Notte), 1522–30
Oil on wood, 101 x 74" (256.5 x 188 cm)
Gemäldegalerie Alte Meister—Staatliche
Kunstsammlungen Dresden

124

Federico Barocci (ca. 1535–1612)
The Madonna del Popolo, 1574–78
Oil on wood, 141⅜ x 99¼" (359 x 252 cm)
Galleria degli Uffizi, Florence

OPPOSITE:
Parmigianino (1503–1540)
Madonna of the Long Neck, ca. 1535
Oil on wood, 85 x 52" (216 x 132 cm)
Galleria degli Uffizi, Florence

Ludovico Carracci (1555–1619)
The Madonna degli Scalzi, ca. 1590
Oil on canvas, 86¼ x 56⅝" (219 x 144 cm)
Pinacoteca Nazionale, Bologna

Guercino (1591–1666)
A Miracle of San Carlo Borromeo, ca. 1613–14
Oil on canvas, 85⅜ x 46" (217 x 117 cm)
Parish church of San Sebastiano, Renazzo di Cento

Guido Cagnacci (1601–1663)
Martha Rebuking Mary for Her Vanity (The Conversion of Mary Magdalen), ca. 1655–59
Oil on canvas, 90¼ x 104¾" (229 x 265 cm)
Norton Simon Art Foundation

OPPOSITE:
Ubaldo Gandolfi (1728–1781)
Mercury Lulling Argus to Sleep, early 1770s
Oil on canvas, 86 x 53⅝" (218.4 x 136.9 cm)
North Carolina Museum of Art, Raleigh
Purchased with funds from the North
Carolina Art Society in memory of Robert
Lee Humber

12.
The Triumph of Rome

Painting in Rome from Raphael and
Michelangelo to Carlo Maratta

As the *caput mundi*—the center of the ancient world—Rome had been the dominant cultural and artistic force on the Italian peninsula. That as the center of Christendom, it should have continued to play a primary role in the development of Italian painting was to be expected. And, indeed, in the late thirteenth century Jacopo Torriti and Pietro Cavallini were in the vanguard of artistic innovation, alongside the Florentines Cimabue and Giotto (see chapter 4). However, in 1309 the Papacy abandoned Rome for Avignon, initiating the so-called Babylonian captivity, which lasted until 1377. Only in 1420 did Martin V definitively reestablish Rome as the papal city. What he found was a far cry from the grand ancient metropolis. Depopulated, torn by warring factions, her population preyed upon by brigands in the countryside, the city was scarcely fit to live in. Moreover, the great early Christian basilicas were in a state of alarming disrepair. Not until the last quarter of the fifteenth century, following years of intense building activity, did the city begin to recover some of her former stature. It is hardly surprising that between the early fourteenth century and the early sixteenth, no local artist of note emerged (the leading painter of the fifteenth century, Antoniazzo Romano, is scarcely worth mentioning). Rather, when an important task was at hand, artists were brought in from other regions. From Gentile da Fabriano and Masaccio down to Raphael and Michelangelo, almost every major central Italian painter spent some time in Rome working for one or another pope. This pattern was repeated through the eighteenth century. Like Paris in the nineteenth and twentieth centuries, Rome became a magnet for artists but seldom produced any outstanding local personality: the two most notable exceptions, Raphael's pupil Giulio Romano in the sixteenth century and Andrea Sacchi in the seventeenth, prove the rule.

If, however, there was a dearth of local talent, it would be wrong to assume that there was no such thing as a distinctly Roman school or that Rome was anything less than it pretended to be: the artistic capital of the world. The critic Giovanni Battista Agucchi, writing in the early seventeenth century, correctly pinpointed the origins of the Roman school in Raphael and Michelangelo, "who followed the beauty revealed in [Roman] sculpture and came close to the artistry of the Ancients." In Florence, Michelangelo had painted that masterpiece of *disegno,* in which color is the handmaid of sculptural qualities communicated through a mastery of drawing: the *Doni Tondo* (see chapter 8). In Rome, his work acquired a new scale and perfection in direct emulation of the sculpture of antiquity. He created a superhuman race that was to be emulated in painting academies throughout Europe down to the mid-nineteenth century, when Courbet dealt that ideal a fatal blow. In Michelangelo's hands, Adam ceased to be Everyman, becoming, instead, the ideal father of us all, perfect in all but moral judgment.

In a similar fashion, the figures that Raphael painted in Rome shed the sweetness that had characterized his work in Perugia and Florence and acquired a nobility and grace of even greater importance for later artists than the example provided by Michelangelo's frescoes. Many artists before Raphael had been compared to the fabled ancient painter Apelles, but Raphael's *Galatea* was the first that could, legitimately, be compared to the ancient master's renowned painting of Aphrodite rising from the sea for its miraculously effortless-seeming elegance and grace.

Annibale Carracci arrived in Rome in 1595. He was committed to a tradition of northern Italian naturalism (see chapter 11), but faced with the achievement of Michelangelo and the ruins of ancient Rome, he changed course and became the spokesman for a reformed classicism, to which his pupil the

Bolognese painter Domenichino, as well as the resident French artist Poussin and the native Roman Andrea Sacchi, also adhered. So remarkable was the change in Annibale's work that it initiated a dispute over whether the pictures he painted in Bologna or those he did in Rome were greater. To Jacques-Louis David, who shed the last traces of French rococo and unveiled his *Oath of the Horatii* (Musée du Louvre, Paris) in Rome in 1785, there would have been no question; nor would David have hesitated to acknowledge the psychological pull Rome exerted (he had taken his composition to Rome to finish, convinced that only in the cradle of the ancient world could he produce an authentically classical work).

Even that so-called realist Caravaggio was unable to resist the twin legacy of ancient and High Renaissance Rome. His *Cupid Triumphant (Amor vincit omnia)* (Gemäldegalerie, Berlin) pays homage both to the tradition of the male nude championed by Michelangelo and to the refined beauty of Hellenistic sculpture, but it recasts these illustrious prototypes from nature, using as a model a twelve-year-old youth who seems also to have been Caravaggio's lover. His celebrated *Entombment* (Vatican Museums) has the cadence and restraint of a classical relief, but again given a new expressive force and vitality through the use of actual models.

In the 1480s painters had found a passage into the buried wonders of the Golden House of Nero, and those who visited the city made the obligatory descent by torchlight, copying onto scraps of paper the patterns from the frescoed vaults (which became known as *grotteschi*, or grottesques, from the grottolike appearance of the dirt-filled rooms). The Umbrian painter Pintoricchio was among the first to explore the excavations, translating the designs he saw onto the walls of Alexander Borgia's apartments in the Vatican. By the early sixteenth century, other Roman frescoes were also unearthed, and the technique of Roman painting was being imitated by Raphael's pupil Polidoro da Caravaggio. The background of Giulio Romano's altarpiece in Santa Maria dell'Anima is enlivened with reminiscences of Roman ruins, and throughout the sixteenth century, much painting in Rome aspired to the quality of marble sculpture. For the generation of Poussin, the ancient Roman fresco of the so-called *Aldobrandini Wedding* (named for the family who owned the fresco) exerted a special appeal and encouraged his preference for friezelike compositions.

The concomitant of this obsession with ancient art was the promotion of art theory and criticism, reaching a high point in the work of Giovanni Pietro Bellori, whose *Lives* were published in 1672. The writings of ancient authors (foremost among them Aristotle and Horace), and their concern for decorum and expressivity achieved through a careful study of gesture, are the underpinnings of Domenichino's fresco of Saint Cecilia distributing her wealth, in which the classically conceived architecture serves as a stage setting for the action. And it is a Platonic belief in the existence of a higher realm of ideal beauty that pervades the religious work of Andrea Sacchi and his pupil Carlo Maratta. Academic teaching may be said to have its mainspring in the Carracci reform in Bologna (see chapter 11), with its emphasis on drawing from nature, and its paradigm in Rome, where the great works of the past guided artists in their quest for perfection.

Michelangelo (1475–1564)
The Tempation and Fall of Man, 1508–12
Fresco
Sistine Chapel, Vatican
Copyright Nippon Television Network
Corporation Tokyo 1991

Michelangelo (1475–1564)
The Erythrean Sibyl, 1508–12
Fresco
Sistine Chapel, Vatican
Copyright Nippon Television Network
Corporation Tokyo 1991

OPPOSITE:
Raphael (1483–1520)
Triumph of Galatea, ca. 1511–13
Fresco
Villa Farnesina, Rome

Francesco Salviati (1510–1563)
The Visitation, 1538
Fresco
Oratorio di San Giovanni Decollato, Rome

OPPOSITE:
Sebastiano del Piombo (ca. 1485–1547)
Pietà, 1514
Oil on wood, 106¼ x 88½" (270 x 225 cm)
Museo Civico, Viterbo

Domenichino (1581–1641)
Saint Cecilia Distributing Her Wealth to the Poor, 1611–14
Fresco
San Luigi dei Francesi, Rome

OPPOSITE:
Carlo Maratta (1625–1713)
Madonna and Child with Angels and Saints, 1685
Oil on canvas
Santa Maria in Vallicella, Rome

140

Andrea Sacchi (1599/1600–1655)
Hagar and Ishmael in the Wilderness, ca. 1630
Oil on canvas, 36½ x 37¾" (92 x 96 cm)
National Museum of Wales, Cardiff

13.
The Hard Edge of Reality

Painting in Naples in the 15th–18th centuries

Naples holds a special place among Italian cities. Its origins were Greek, not Etruscan or Roman, and throughout its history it was subject to foreign rule. In the Middle Ages it formed part of the Byzantine Empire until conquered by the Normans in 1139, when it became part of the Kingdom of Sicily. Subsequently, it was ruled by the Angevins of France and the Spanish house of Aragón. In 1503 it became directly subject to the Spanish crown and was ruled by a viceroy until 1707. Only in 1734 did it become an autonomous kingdom under a branch of the Bourbon dynasty. By the end of the sixteenth century it was among the largest cities in Europe, exceeded in size only by Paris. Even after a devastating plague in 1656 reduced the population by half, it remained a large and important urban center. It charmed northern visitors, from Brueghel in the sixteenth century to Goethe in the eighteenth. Stendhal, who visited Naples in 1811–12, declared it the only Italian city with "the true makings of a capital."

In the fourteenth century the Florentines Giotto and Maso di Banco, the Sienese Simone Martini, and the Roman Pietro Cavallini all worked in Naples. It is Giotto's shadow that falls across the work of the local painter Roberto d'Oderisio, but there are other pictures for which it is not always possible to state whether they were painted in Naples or in France, under the influence of Simone Martini.

The habit of importing artistic talent continued into the fifteenth century, when works were commissioned from the Lombard painter Leonardo da Besozzo, the Florentines Donatello, Filippo Lippi, and Giuliano da Majano, the Sienese architect-engineer and sculptor Francesco di Giorgio, and the Veronese painter Pisanello. Alfonso of Aragón, who took control of Naples in 1442, particularly prized Flemish painting, of which he owned an outstanding collection, and the one true native genius, Colantonio, worked in a style manifestly derived from Flemish practice. The medium Colantonio employed appears to have been oil rather than the egg tempera common to Italian painting at the time, and the remarkable still-life details he included in works like the *Saint Jerome in His Study* were calculated to appeal to an audience responsive to the representational powers of Flemish artists. Colantonio was the first Neapolitan painter of more than local interest, for through his pupil Antonello da Messina, who was active in Venice in 1475–76, a Flemicizing approach to painting entered the mainstream of Italian art. Curiously, no Neapolitan artist of Colantonio's stature emerged again before the seventeenth century, despite the presence in the city of Raphael's gifted and highly individual pupil Polidoro da Caravaggio. The sudden flowering of Neapolitan painting followed in the wake of Polidoro's countryman Caravaggio, who made two short visits to the city in 1606–7 and 1609–10.

Caravaggio arrived in Naples following the murder in Rome of a tennis opponent. He was at the height of his powers and the most famous painter in Italy. Not surprisingly, Neapolitan patrons were quick to take advantage of his presence. Perhaps his greatest Neapolitan masterpiece was the *Seven Acts of Mercy* he undertook for a charitable foundation, the Pio Monte della Misericordia. It shows the Virgin and her infant son protectively borne aloft by two angels who have burst into a dark, congested backstreet of Naples. The seven acts of mercy referred to in a sermon of Christ's are shown in vivid though abbreviated and emblematic form: healing the sick, burying the dead, visiting the imprisoned, feeding the hungry, giving drink to the thirsty, clothing the naked, and sheltering strangers. The work is astonishing not for its narrative or spatial clarity—indeed, much of the composition is difficult to read and the actions of some of the figures are allusive to the point of being enigmatic—but for the vivid quality of actuality: the plebeian beauty of the woman who offers her breast to an old man behind bars; the juxtaposition of a naked beggar, a young dandy, and a devout pilgrim; and the electrifying presence of the common-featured Virgin and Child who confer their protection. These features struck a deep chord among Neapolitan artists.

Although other "foreign" painters also received commissions in the city—most notably Giovanni Lanfranco, Domenichino, and Guido Reni, all of whom had been pupils of Annibale Carracci in Rome— it was Caravaggio's art, with its hard edge of reality, that dominated Neapolitan painting. Whereas Caravaggism in Rome was a relatively short-lived affair—by 1620 it was all but spent—in Naples it can be traced into the eighteenth century, when it resurfaced in the biting genre scenes of Gaspare Traversi (see chapter 25).

Caravaggio's greatest successor was Jusepe de Ribera, a Spaniard by birth but Italian by training and an almost continuous resident in Naples from 1616 until his death in 1652. Ribera shared Caravaggio's hostile temper, successfully terrorizing Domenichino, who had received the prestigious commission to decorate the chapel of Naples's patron saint, San Gennaro, in the cathedral (Ribera eventually supplanted Domenichino). To Caravaggio's dramatic use of light Ribera added a texturally rich brushwork that confers on even mythological figures a purposefully coarse realism, as in his grotesque *Drunken Silenus*. His pictures are conceived in an ironic spirit that did not, however, preclude a real feeling for beauty, particularly evident in his dark-eyed young Madonnas.

A sense of irony may seem an individual rather than regional trait, but in Naples it seems to have become a standard means of survival, resurfacing in countless works: in the disquieting detail of the severed hands of an infant in Massimo Stanzione's *Massacre of the Innocents*, or in Salvator Rosa's macabre treatment of an allegory of human frailty.

Yet, not all Caravaggesque art was born of the streets. Bernardo Cavallino's paintings are conspicuous for their refined timbre and Mattia Preti's for their fluid bravura. Bravura is the other side of Neapolitan art, and it was finely tuned by that most prolific of artists, Luca Giordano, who was capable of counterfeiting Ribera's realism or of painting works with the dazzling technical flourish of a fireworks display. Only in the art carried out for the Bourbon court in the eighteenth century by painters like Francesco de Mura does this marvelously extravagant art yield to a more conventional notion of good taste.

Caravaggio (1571–1610)
Seven Acts of Mercy, 1606/7
Oil on canvas, 153½ x 102⅜" (390 x 260 cm)
Pio Monte della Misericordia, Naples

Colantonio (active between 1440 and ca. 1470)
Saint Jerome in His Study, ca. 1460–70
Oil on wood, 49¼ x 59" (125 x 150 cm)
Gallerie Nazionali di Capodimonte, Naples

Jusepe de Ribera (1591–1652)
Drunken Silenus, 1626
Oil on canvas, 72⅞ x 90⅛" (185 x 229 cm)
Gallerie Nazionali di Capodimonte, Naples

Bernardo Cavallino (1616–1656)
The Shade of Samuel Invoked by Saul, ca. 1650–56
Oil on copper, 24 x 34" (61 x 86.5 cm)
The J. Paul Getty Museum, Malibu, California

Salvator Rosa (1615–1673)
Human Fragility, ca. 1656
Oil on canvas, 73½ x 52⅜" (186.5 x 133 cm)
The Fitzwilliam Museum, Cambridge

Luca Giordano (1634–1705)
Saint Tommaso da Villanova Distributing Alms, 1658
Oil on canvas, 138 x 90½" (350 x 230 cm)
Sant'Agostino degli Scalzi, Naples

150

Mattia Preti (1613–1699)
The Feast of Herod, 1656–61
Oil on canvas, 70 x 99¼" (177.8 x 252.1 cm)
The Toledo Museum of Art, Toledo, Ohio
Purchased with funds from the Libbey Endowment;
Gift of Edward Drummond Libbey

Francesco Solimena (1657–1747)
Heliodorus Expelled from the Temple, ca. 1725
Oil on canvas, 60 x 80¼" (152.4 x 203.8 cm)
The Toledo Museum of Art, Toledo, Ohio
Purchased with funds from the Libbey Endowment;
Gift of Edward Drummond Libbey

I4.
Stretching Space

Illusionistic painting from the age of Giotto to the age of Tiepolo

From the vantage point of the late twentieth century, following the hard-won victories of abstract art against the traditions of academic painting, it has become fashionable to treat Renaissance art patronizingly as the misconceived offspring of Art and Science fostered by a hopelessly positivist society—as though abstraction were a purer expressive language and the result of a higher calling. Abstraction is, of course, innate to all art, whether representational or nonrepresentational. However, although representational art has flourished in every culture, only in ancient Greece and Rome and then again in Europe between the fifteenth and the nineteenth centuries was the mastery of the visible world in all its physical aspects made its principal goal. This mastery depended on two achievements: the ability to impart the appearance of solidity to individual forms—above all the human figure, with which we tend to identify most readily—and the ability to create a convincing spatial setting. Either faculty can exist independently, and although the humanist vision of painting first put forward in Leon Battista Alberti's landmark treatise on painting of 1435 required both, some of the most surprising and idiosyncratic achievements of Western art derived from the ability to stretch the physical space we inhabit onto the most improbable surfaces: the wall or ceiling of a room or the curved, inner surface of a dome elevated high above the viewer's head.

It was Giotto who first realized the necessity of creating a cogent spatial stage for the action of his weighty figures (see chapter 5) and who also first delighted in his newfound ability to suggest pure, architectural spaces that challenge the viewer's sense of reality. In the Arena Chapel in Padua (the building housing his greatest fresco cycle depicting the life of the Virgin Mary and of Christ), he created a fictive chamber to either side of the actual apse, shown as though viewed through an arched opening, the back wall pierced by a delicate biforate window, the ribbed vaults painted blue, with a hanging chandelier to which are attached oil lamps. The theory of perspective had not yet been codified, and Giotto had to rely upon an empirical approach finely tuned by his remarkable eye. Nonetheless, this tour de force established a means by which later artists could measure their mastery of art and their ability to deceive the eye.

Sometimes the object of attention was a trompe l'oeil cabinet stocked with communion utensils on the wall of a chapel or a fictive bench pushed up against the wall. At other times it was a more ambitious scheme in which the irregular shape of a wall was integrated into the pictorial scheme, as occurs in Lippo Vanni's fresco of the Annunciation in the ex-hermitage of San Leonardo al Lago, near Siena, in which the rooms housing the angel Gabriel and the Virgin are made to wrap around the window embrasure.

The discovery of perspective—the ability to re-create mathematically our experience of space—belongs not to a painter but to an architect, Filippo Brunelleschi. It seems to have been the outgrowth of making elaborate, measured drawings of buildings. However, it was Brunelleschi's young friend Masaccio who around 1425 first applied perspective to a figurative composition, using it to confer an astonishing quality of reality on the depiction of a theological concept. In his fresco of the Trinity, God the father, the crucified Christ, and the dove of the Holy Spirit inhabit a Renaissance chapel that stretches the space of the viewer standing in the Gothic nave of Santa Maria Novella in Florence into an imaginary but plausible realm. This illusion is complemented by portraits of the husband and wife who commissioned the fresco kneeling in front of their fictive chapel, within the viewer's own space.

It was this use of perspective as an agent in bringing the divine down to earth that gained widespread application in a number of Renaissance frescoes and altarpieces, sometimes with real framing elements used to further obfuscate the division between the world of the imagined from that we live in—as in a number of altarpieces by Giovanni Bellini, and Raphael's famous *Sistine Madonna*, which was meant to be seen through a carved frame, with the painted curtains drawn back to reveal the heavenly vision beyond and the two cherubs leaning on the lower ledge. In Andrea del Sarto's fresco of the Last Supper in the refectory of San Salvi, Florence, the space of the viewer appears to have been extended back another bay and the architecture made more grand.

Once it was realized that walls offered no resistance to the new spatial science, it was only a matter of time before ceilings were also opened up. This first happened in a private room in the Gonzaga's castle in Mantua, where Andrea Mantegna transformed with his brush an ordinary plaster ceiling into a richly carved one with marble medallions of the Caesars backed with feigned gold mosaics. At the center Mantegna punched a fictive hole—a balcony—over which members of the Gonzaga court and their a saucy peacock peer down at the spectator. As a final touch to this exuberant display, he added a potted plant that threatens to plunge into the viewer's space.

Mantegna's conceit was the basis of the illusionistic vaults realized by his pupil Correggio, who discarded architectural accouterments in favor of a purely figurative illusionism. His dome in San Giovanni Evangelista in Parma became, in turn, the reference point for those great baroque empyreans that decorate so many churches throughout Italy. Perhaps the most breathtaking of all of these opened ceiling spaces is Tiepolo's monumental fresco above the grand staircase of the Residenz in Wurzburg, showing Apollo and the planets against an seemingly endless expanse of sky. As in Mantegna's fresco, most of the figures are firmly massed around the architectural cornice, while isolated groups are strung in a continuous chain that spirals into the cloud-swept space.

The opposite approach, in which feigned architecture and sculpture are used to articulate and aggrandize a vast expanse of ceiling, was espoused by Michelangelo in the Sistine Chapel (see chapter 12). Michelangelo sought to create an architectural framework for his biblical scenes, rather than to abolish the surface on which he painted, and in the ceiling, figurative elements are used to sustain the illusionistic coherence of the architecture. No one understood the conceit better than Annibale Carracci, whose ceiling in the Palazzo Farnese in Rome, completed almost ninety years later, was a direct homage to Michelangelo, but with a new, playful spirit. Carracci's work includes both feigned marble sculpture, some of it broken so as to look old, and feigned human figures perched on the cornice. It was common for artists faced with this sort of task to employ specialists in architectural painting who could set the stage, so to speak, for the figurative elements. This was the case with Guercino's ceiling in the Casino Ludovisi in Rome showing an allegorical figure of Dawn, in which the fictive architecture was painted by Agostino Tassi. On the other hand, Pietro da Cortona painted the crumbling architecture and the figures on the vault in Palazzo Barberini, as did Andrea Pozzo in that most extravagant tour de force of illusionistic ceiling painting in the church of Sant'Ignazio, Rome. Pozzo was an accomplished mathematician, and his ceiling can only be fully appreciated from a single vanishing point, conveniently marked in the inlaid marble pavement of the church.

There are, finally, those marvelous exercises in pure illusionism—as powerfully intellectual and dazzling as any abstract work of art—by which whole rooms are magically transformed. Baldassare Peruzzi's Room of Perspectives in the Villa Farnesina, painted in 1518–19, is perhaps the most conspicuous case: a feat of illusionism that is more effective than anything surviving from ancient Rome. At Villa Maser, north of Padua, Veronese also vied with the purported mastery of ancient artists to create a fictive realm, complete with landscape views and an occasional pet or child peeking through a partly opened door. And in the hands of that genial Merlin Giambattista Tiepolo (who employed an architectural specialist, Mengozzi-Colonna) not only space but time is stretched, as a resplendent Cleopatra prepares to descend into the room the viewer stands in. In this elevated work two realities confront each other, each in its own way complete, but one answerable to laws dictated by the artist, who assumes a godlike status as creator of his own universe.

Giotto (1266–1337)
Interior of Arena Chapel (detail), ca. 1304–6
Fresco
Arena Chapel, Padua

OPPOSITE:
Giotto (1266–1337)
Interior of Arena Chapel
(Cappella degli Scrovegni), ca. 1304–6
Fresco
Arena Chapel, Padua

Masaccio (1401–1428)
Trinity, ca. 1425–27
Fresco, 262½ (including base)
x 125" (667 x 317 cm)
Santa Maria Novella, Florence

159

Andrea del Sarto (1486–1530)
Last Supper, 1522—27
Fresco
San Salvi, Florence

OPPOSITE:
Giovanni Bellini
Madonna and Child with Saints, 1505
Oil on wood, 206 x 92½" (523 x 235 cm)
San Zaccaria, Venice

OPPOSITE:
Andrea Mantegna (ca. 1430–1506)
Ceiling of the Camera degli Sposi, ca. 1464
Fresco
Palazzo Ducale, Mantua

Correggio (ca. 1489–1534)
Dome of San Giovanni Evangelista, ca. 1520–23
Fresco
San Giovanni Evangelista, Parma

165

Giovanni Lanfranco (1582–1647)
Dome of Sant'Andrea della Valle, 1625–27
with pendentives and vault by
Domenichino (1581-1641)
Fresco
Sant'Andrea della Valle, Rome

OPPOSITE:
Bacciccio (1639–1709)
Triumph of the Name of Jesus, 1672–85
Fresco
Il Gesù, Rome

Guercino (1591–1666)
Dawn, 1621
Fresco
Casino Ludovisi, Rome

OPPOSITE TOP:
Andrea Pozzo (1642–1709)
Glory of Saint Ignatius Loyola, after 1685
Fresco
Sant'Ignazio, Rome

OPPOSITE BOTTOM:
Pietro da Cortona (1596–1669)
Triumph of Divine Providence, 1638–39
Fresco
Palazzo Barberini, Rome

Baldassare Peruzzi (1481–1536)
Sala delle Prospettive, 1518–19
Fresco
Villa Farnesina, Rome

Paolo Veronese (1528–1588)
Stanza del Cane, ca. 1559–60
Fresco
Villa Maser

OPPOSITE:
Giambattista Tiepolo (1696–1770)
Arrival of Cleopatra, ca. 1746
Fresco
Palazzo Labia, Venice

15.
Painting as Poetry
The origins of history painting in the 15th–17th centuries

In his treatise on the art of poetry, the ancient writer Horace remarked that "a poem is like a picture: one strikes your fancy more the nearer you stand to it, another when farther away. This one courts the shade while that one must be seen in the light and does not shrink from the critical insight of the judge. . . ." Seized upon by Renaissance thinkers obsessed with culling whatever information Greek and Roman writers thought about art, this seemingly casual observation was elevated to the center of humanist criticism. In the middle of the fifteenth century Bartolomeo Fazio alluded to it and to similar comparisons between poetry and painting made by ancient authors when he noted, "there is, as you know, a great affinity between painters and poets: a painting is indeed nothing else but a wordless poem."

At the time, Fazio was historian and secretary to Alfonso of Aragón in Naples, but prior to 1440 he had been in touch with humanist circles in Florence and northern Italy, and his views were widely shared. Especially at the court of Lionello d'Este in Ferrara these literary-biased ideas about painting were developed with great cogency. At a time when the most fashionable kind of poetry was one emphasizing the author's prowess at elaborate description and when command of language involved what we would consider linguistic gymnastics, it is hardly surprising that the most admired pictures were those displaying a predisposition to detailed naturalism. In Ferrara the Flemish artist Rogier van der Weyden and the northern Italian Pisanello were much in vogue. Fazio, too, singles out these painters together with Jan van Eyck and Gentile da Fabriano (but not, interestingly enough, Masaccio). It was the abundant and carefully observed details in these artists' paintings that critics responded to.

Gentile da Fabriano's masterpiece, the *Adoration of the Magi,* was painted in 1423 for the wealthiest citizen of Florence, Palla Strozzi, who was also a leading supporter of humanist studies. There can be no doubt that the marvelous details that fill every inch—the lunette scenes showing the Wise Men sighting the star on a hill next to a vast sea, their journey across a Tuscan-inspired landscape, and their entry into the starlit city of Bethlehem—was conceived as a visual counterpart to the sorts of literary exercises Palla Strozzi must have composed in his moments of leisure. In this sense, Gentile's work is anything but representative of the so-called International Gothic Style—usually thought of as the antithesis of the Renaissance style of Masaccio. Rather, it is humanist in inspiration, however different its visual vocabulary might seem to us.

This narrow literary view lies behind a number of remarkable pictures, foremost among which is Pisanello's well-known fresco of *Saint George and the Princess of Trebizond,* with its inclusion of carefully studied horses, exotically dressed Mongols, and a landscape notable for the grisly detail of figures hanging from gallows. Indicatively, Pisanello signed the fresco with beautiful capital letters taken from inscriptions on Roman monuments: a detail certain to please his educated audience. Jacopo Bellini's *Madonna and Child,* with its equally detailed background (especially notable for the depiction of a sunrise), was painted for Lionello d'Este, who is shown kneeling in the foreground. Perhaps no one developed the potential of this sort of painting further than Cosimo Tura (see chapter 7), in whose convoluted compositions and eccentrically agitated figures we recognize a visual analogue to a fine, literary turn of phrase or the use of a self-consciously elaborate sentence construction.

A more fruitful and enduring critical approach was developed by that man of all trades (writer, theorist, mathematician, and architect), Leon Battista Alberti, who in 1435 composed what remains the most influential treatise on painting ever written. In it Alberti not only laid down the theory of one-point perspective but first conceived of the learned painter: someone with a strong grounding in the liberal arts who took as his greatest task the illustration of a story or legend (what Alberti called an "historia," or history painting). Alberti's reading of classical authors was perhaps wider than that of any other Renaissance writer on art, and he evolved his theories from classical notions of diction and rhetoric, and from Aristotle's comments on the principles governing staged drama. Alberti remembered Lucian's description of a painting by the great Greek painter Apelles that showed an allegory of Calumny in which figures of Ignorance and Suspicion filled the ears of an ass-eared man sitting in judgment of a youth falsely accused by Calumny and Envy, while Truth stood by unheeded. Needless to say, a number of artists took inspiration from Alberti's description, including Botticelli, whose painting of the *Calumny of Apelles* (Galleria degli Uffizi, Florence) was not only an attempt to revive a kind of painting current in ancient Greece and Rome, but also an exercise in the new narrative style emphasizing clarity of statement allied to a subject of high moral interest.

Alberti's ideas were developed over the course of the next three centuries in a variety of ways, and without some understanding of and sympathy for the ideas he put forward, it is impossible to fully appreciate the works of such great European masters as Domenichino, Poussin, or David, with their attempts to use painting as a vehicle for communicating ideas, their interest in formulating gesture as a means of conveying emotion (what came to be called the "affetti"), and their attempts to create compositions that could be "read" as clearly as one might read a text. Today, when artists are frequently concerned with defining the nature of Art, the idea that it could find fulfillment as illustration seems both perverse and degrading. And yet, the masterpieces inspired by the Renaissance notion of history painting, with its emphasis on painting as an intellectual discipline, belies this verdict.

Raphael's fresco of the *Fire in the Borgo* and his altarpiece of the *Transfiguration* as well as Domenichino's *Last Communion of Saint Jerome* are great works of art not despite the stories they illustrate, but because of the qualities of mind and invention and the facility of hand that have been brought to bear on a story that may or may not be of interest to the viewer. Until well into the nineteenth century Raphael's *Transfiguration,* in which the miraculous transfiguration of Christ on Mount Tabor is contrasted with the inability of his disciples to heal an obsessed youth, and Domenichino's *Last Communion of Saint Jerome,* in which the devotion of the old ascetic is described with affective nobility, were widely considered the twin peaks of European painting. In them the artists were felt to have fully realized what for Alberti was the highest goal of art: "to move the eyes and heart of the viewer."

174

Gentile da Fabriano (ca. 1380–1427)
The Adoration of the Magi, 1423
Tempera and gold on wood, 118⅛ x 111"
(300 x 282 cm)
Galleria degli Uffizi, Florence

SANCTVS·GIORGIVS·

Pisanello (ca. 1390–1455)
*Saint George and the Princess of
Trebizond*, ca. 1436–38
Fresco
Sant'Anastasia, Verona

OPPOSITE:
Jacopo Bellini (ca. 1400–1470)
Madonna and Child with Lionello d'Este, ca. 1440
Tempera and gold on wood,
23⅝ x 15¾" (60 x 40 cm)
Musée du Louvre, Paris

176

Perugino (1445/50–1523)
Christ Giving the Keys to Saint Peter, 1482
Fresco
Sistine Chapel, Vatican

Raphael (1483–1520)
The Transfiguration, 1518–20
Oil on wood, 159½ x 109½" (405 x 278 cm)
Pinacoteca Vaticana, Vatican

Domenichino (1581–1641)
The Last Communion of Saint Jerome, 1614
Oil on canvas, 165 x 100¾" (419 x 256 cm)
Pinacoteca Vaticana, Vatican

OPPOSITE:
Guido Reni (1575–1642)
The Massacre of the Innocents, 1611–12
Oil on canvas, 105½ x 67" (268 x 170 cm)
Pinacoteca Nazionale, Bologna

16.
Venus, Love, and Poetry
Mythological painting in the 15ᵗʰ–18ᵗʰ centuries

"Be praised, my Lord, for sister moon and the stars. In heaven you have made them clear and precious and lovely," sings Saint Francis in his unsurpassed paean of praise, the *Canticle of All Created Things*. When, in the early thirteenth century, he wrote these words, the moon as a symbol of the vagaries of sensual love or as the ensign of the virgin goddess Diana could not have been further from his mind. Petrarch's exclamation to his beloved, "In what part of heaven, in what celestial form was the original from which Nature took that glad, lovely face?" was still a century away.

It is a commonplace that the raptures experienced by religious mystics resemble to a surprising degree the sensual pleasures of lovers in their first embrace, and a good deal of courtly etiquette was directed to heightening the experience of love by formalizing the steps leading to its consummation, or by prolonging the morbid excitement of anticipation by making it all but unobtainable or unrequited. When that crowning figure of fifteenth-century Medicean Florence, the poet Angelo Poliziano, declared, "I thank you, Love, for every pain and torment, and am happy now for your every sorrow," he might almost be thought an ascetic seeking salvation through the rigors of Christian penitence rather than a votary of Venus, habituated to the disdain of the beloved that was one of the hallmarks of courtly love as evolved in medieval France and refined in the Neoplatonic circles of Renaissance Florence.

In Renaissance Italy, alongside the carefully tended garden of the Madonna, another, more densely planted and elaborately pruned park was laid out for the pleasures of Venus, who shared with her Christian counterpart the rose as her emblem (it was to a mystical white rose floating in the empyrean that Dante was led by his beloved Beatrice to behold the heavenly host and their queen, the Virgin Mary). In such a garden, perfumed by ripening oranges, the heroes of chivalric lore—Achilles, Tristan, Lancelot, Samson, Paris, and Troilus—are shown kneeling in rapt devotion before an apparition of the goddess Venus in an early fifteenth-century Florentine painting (Musée du Louvre, Paris). The ancient goddess appears, like the Madonna, in a golden mandorla, attended by two claw-footed cupids the color of seraphs. She is shown winged, like an angel, and crowned, like the queen of heaven. It is recounted that Saint Bernard was granted the singular rapture of tasting the milk from the Virgin Mary's breast, but the golden rays that inspire these devotees of love emanate from Venus's genitals.

"Welcome, Spring, that desires man to fall in love, and you, maidens, in a crowd with your lovers, who make yourselves lovely with roses and other flowers in May, come to the cool shade of the green bushes." The picture conjured up by these verses of Poliziano is the painting we now know as the *Primavera*, or *Springtime*, in which Botticelli appropriates the mood of Poliziano's poetry to evoke the realm of Venus, subject to the capriciousness of a blindfolded Cupid who shoots his flaming arrows indiscriminately. Maying was one of the great pleasures of courtly life, and it is Spring that Venus claimed as her season. At the right in Botticelli's picture the nymph Chloris is transformed by the gentle west wind, Zephyr, into Flora, the goddess of Springtime, who scatters her flowers throughout the orange grove. To the left the Graces weave an elegant dance while Mercury dissipates any clouds. It has been argued that Botticelli's painting, created for Lorenzo the Magnificent's second cousin Lorenzo di Pierfrancesco de'Medici, is a Neoplatonic rebus based on a program drawn up by the Medicean philosopher Marsilio Ficino, or that it is a direct translation into visual terms of Poliziano's stanzas composed following a celebrated joust (the *Giostra*). What the painting shares with Poliziano and, indeed, with those ancient poets who inspired his verse, is a mood of heavy luxuriance. Venus has not yet shed those angular features so prized by Gothic artists, and in conformity with Ficino's ideas of chaste love, her features are still those

Botticelli conferred on his depictions of the Madonna (see chapter 8), but there is no doubt that the pleasures she inspires are sensual in nature.

In the late 1470s, when Botticelli's picture was created, Venus had assumed a central place in the lives of well-born Florentines. Roman poets had practiced a genre of poetry in celebration of newlyweds of which Venus was the subject and her object the blessing of the bride, on whom she conferred the promise of fertility and happiness. As the goddess of matrimonial bliss, a figure of the reclining Venus is sometimes found on the insides of lids of marriage chests (*cassone*), usually paired with a depiction of the shepherd Paris who awarded her the golden apple (thereby precipitating the Trojan War). This genre of poetry (epithalamia) was revived by Renaissance poets and inspired some of the most famous images of Venus. Indeed, the recitation of epithalamia at weddings became common practice, and images of Venus, alone or conquering the martial god Mars, became the decoration of choice for wedding chambers (the Florentine picture of the worthies worshiping Venus, described above, was painted as a tray to celebrate the birth of a child, while Botticelli's *Primavera* was designed to sit above a daybed). Giorgione's celebrated painting of the *Sleeping Venus* (Gemäldegalerie, Dresden) was, in all likelihood, painted for the marriage of the Venetian Girolamo Marcello in 1507, and Annibale Carracci's splendid painting at Chantilly, in which cupids play at dressing up (a mock wedding is enacted by two naughty cupids at the right) while Venus sleeps on a draped couch, was clearly painted as a visual epithalamium and must have been destined for a couple of high social standing.

Of all those marriage pictures that have come down to us, none is more singular than that painted by the Venetian contemporary of Titian, Lorenzo Lotto, in the 1520s. In it Venus, her head adorned with a crown and veil like those worn by aristocratic brides, reclines beneath a tree on which ivy, symbol of undying devotion, climbs. The red cloth draped behind the nude figure is the color the ancients preferred for the wedding chamber, while the myrtle wreath and incense burner she holds suspended from a ribbon are, again, accouterments to the nuptial room. Into this idyllic scene Lotto introduced an impudent Cupid, his crown of myrtle jauntily askew, who directs a stream of urine through the wreath his mother holds, onto her lap: an almost shockingly forthright invocation of fertility for the bride whose features this Venus possibly has been given.

The crucial factor in understanding mythological paintings of the Renaissance and baroque periods is not their potentially abstruse symbols, interesting and erudite though they may be, but the attempt to create visual analogues to poetic concepts. Botticelli's *Birth of Venus* consciously evokes the Homeric hymn to Venus and shows the rose-showered goddess blown to the shore, where she is clothed by the Hours. The loves of Jupiter, whether Correggio's depiction of the god, who has assumed the guise of a cloud, ravishing the nymph Io, or Titian's sublime rendition of Juno's lascivious husband making off with Europa, who he had lured on his back disguised as a bull, convert the ancient poet Ovid into images of compelling beauty. Ovid had been translated into Italian and was widely read, and the comic detail in Titian's painting of a cupid roughriding a prickly fish is taken from one of these renditions. The popularity and effectiveness of these pictures were bound up with the study and admiration for classical literature as well as for the talents of the artists who painted them.

At times classical subjects became the basis of a more elaborate allegory. In the case of Dosso Dossi's painting of *Jupiter and Mercury*, Jupiter is shown painting butterflies on clouds while Mercury stands guard. By this story Dosso surely meant to suggest his own representational skills. Moreover, the planets

Jupiter and Mercury, together with the constellation Virgo (suggested by the female at the far right of the composition), provide an astrological diagram for the artist.

Titian's *Sacred and Profane Love*, which was, again, painted for a wedding, depicts the twin Venuses: one clothed, ruling the sensual passions; the other nude, inspiring newlyweds to a higher, more celestial (and unsullied) realm of love. The painting offers a Neoplatonic program in the guise of Venetian courtesans, whose beauty was as celebrated in the sixteenth century as those of Paris were in the nineteenth. Bronzino's famous allegory *Venus, Cupid, and Time* comments on the powers of love, the deceptions of jealousy it inspires, and the inexorable triumph of Time, while employing as its vehicle the incestuous relationship between Venus and her son, shown engaged in a lascivious embrace. Such programs retained their allure down to the eighteenth century, when Pompeo Batoni invented for a patron his own allegory showing father Time instructing his daughter, Old Age, to wreak her ravages on a Roman beauty. Seldom has a moral admonition been clothed so seductively as in these antique-inspired works.

Sandro Botticelli (1445–1510)
Primavera, ca. 1478
Tempera on wood, 80 x 124" (203 x 314 cm)
Galleria degli Uffizi, Florence

Sandro Botticelli (1445–1510)
Birth of Venus, ca. 1482–85
Distemper on canvas, 72¾ x 112½" (184.5 x 285.5 cm)
Galleria degli Uffizi, Florence

Piero di Cosimo (1461/62–1521)
Mars and Venus, ca. 1505
Oil on wood, 28⅜ x 71⅝" (72 x 182 cm)
Gemäldegalerie, Staatliche Museen, Berlin

Lorenzo Lotto (ca. 1480–1556)
Venus and Cupid, ca. 1526
Oil on canvas, 36⅜ x 43⅞" (92.4 x 111.4 cm)
The Metropolitan Museum of Art, New York
Purchase, Mrs. Charles Wrightsman Gift, 1986

OPPOSITE TOP:
Annibale Carracci (1560–1609)
Sleeping Venus, ca. 1600
Oil on canvas, 74¾ x 129⅛" (190 x 328 cm)
Musée Condé, Chantilly

OPPOSITE BOTTOM:
Sebastiano Ricci (1659–1734)
The Toilette of Venus, ca. 1725
Oil on canvas, 43 x 56" (109 x 142 cm)
Gemäldegalerie, Staatliche Museen, Berlin

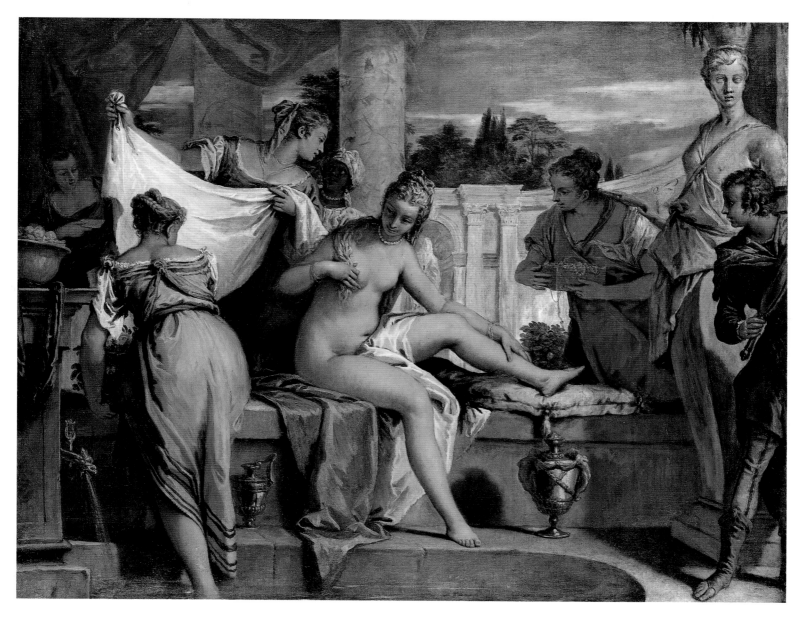

192

Titian (1488/89–1576)
Rape of Europa, 1559–62
Oil on canvas, 72⅞ x 80¾" (185 x 205 cm)
Isabella Stewart Gardner Museum, Boston

OPPOSITE:
Correggio (ca. 1489–1534)
Jupiter and Io, ca. 1531
Oil on canvas, 64⅛ x 28" (163 x 71 cm)
Kunsthistorisches Museum, Vienna

TOP:
Titian (1488/89–1576)
Sacred and Profane Love, ca. 1515
Oil on canvas, 46½ x 109⅞" (118 x 279 cm)
Galleria Borghese, Rome

Dosso Dossi (active by 1512, died 1542)
Jupiter and Mercury, 1529
Oil on canvas, 44⅛ x 59" (112 x 150 cm)
Kunsthistorisches Museum, Vienna

Paolo Veronese (1528–1588)
Mars and Venus, 1570s
Oil on canvas, 81 x 63⅜" (205.7 x 161 cm)
The Metropolitan Museum of Art, New York
John Stewart Kennedy Fund, 1910

Pompeo Batoni (1708–1787)
Time Orders Old Age to Destroy Beauty, 1745–46
Oil on canvas, 53¼ x 38" (135.3 x 96.5 cm)
Reproduced by courtesy of the Trustees,
The National Gallery, London

OPPOSITE:
Agnolo Bronzino (1503–1572)
Venus, Cupid, Time, and Jealousy, ca. 1540–45
Oil on wood, 57½ x 45⅝" (146 x 116 cm)
Reproduced by courtesy of the Trustees,
The National Gallery, London

197

17.
Portraits of Status

Portraiture and society in the ages of the Renaissance
and baroque

To judge from the testimony of ancient authors, such as Pliny, who wrote in the first century A.D., as well
as from surviving examples, portraiture flourished in antiquity. Busts of the emperors stood in public
buildings, their profiles adorned coins, and in private houses it was the custom to display wax effigies of
notable ancestors on sideboards. Additionally, portable painted portraits, "used to transmit through the
ages extremely correct likenesses of persons" (Pliny), were widely produced. Indeed, were one to judge
from the example of ancient Rome alone, it might be thought that portraiture was the most common of
art forms. However, history teaches otherwise, and even Pliny lamented that the practices he recorded had
fallen out of fashion, portraits being then prized more for their authorship and artistic value than as
records of the appearance of an individual. Portraiture as the record of an individual's features is the exception, not the rule. In the Middle Ages it all but disappeared: it was the office of a prince, knight, or king,
not his features, that was imprinted on tomb effigies. Only in the Renaissance does portraiture as the
ancients understood it and as we would recognize it reemerge. Yet even then the balance between the sitter
as an individual and the sitter as occupying a particular station in life is frequently weighted toward the
latter—toward portraits of status.

During the first century and a half of its revival—from roughly 1300 to 1450—the standard formula for a portrait was the profile, the simplest and most efficacious way of recording a person's features.
What we would call individual traits were confined to the shape of the nose or ear or the cut of the hair.
In Pisanello's portrait of Lionello d'Este, the marquis of Ferrara, painted in 1441, the sitter has the
appearance of a rare butterfly specimen that has been carefully pressed and mounted to show its distin-
guishing traits to best advantage. The marquis's sloping forehead and aquiline nose, his sensuous lips and
large, delicate ear—emphasized by the diagonal slash of his haircut—are beautifully played against the
sumptuous brocade of his jacket and the hedge of roses, both of which serve to distance him from an
everyday situation and help create the impression of a sensitive but aloof ruler. It is small wonder that
long after the three-quarter-view portrait head came into fashion, the profile was preferred by rulers and
people of status.

In Ghirlandaio's fresco in the church of Santa Trinità, Florence, showing the *Confirmation of the
Franciscan Rule,* which is filled with portraits of leading citizens of fifteenth-century Florence, Lorenzo the
Magnificent is singled out from his companions at the right by being shown in strict profile, staring ahead
impassively, while his companion, Antonio Pucci, glances out furtively at the viewer.

About 1518 Jacopo Pontormo was commissioned to paint a posthumous dynastic portrait of the
founder of the Medici rulers of Florence, Cosimo il Vecchio, who had died in 1464. The likeness was
based on a portrait medal, which partly explains the use of the profile, by then an archaic form, but
Pontormo plainly relished the opportunity to use this courtly formula, enhanced by the backdrop of laurel branches, to endow the crafty politician—one of the most pragmatic men of his day—with a sensitive,
almost pathological princely mien. As late as the mid-sixteenth century the Florentine poetess Laura
Battiferri had her friend Agnolo Bronzino depict her in profile, holding an open book displaying two
poems by Petrarch, to play up her aristocratic bearing and intellectual character.

It was as a Christian knight, armored, holding a lance, gazing steadily ahead, his horse ready to go
into battle, that Emperor Charles V chose to be portrayed by Titian in 1548, following the defeat of the

Protestant League at Mühlberg. This was a formula that emphasized vigor and resolve rather than abstract thought. Thereafter, the equestrian portrait became associated with royal sitters, who are frequently depicted executing a levade or another of the difficult equine movements promoted by the riding schools of Europe. These riding schools have their origin in Renaissance Italy: typically, the earliest and most influential book on riding, published in Naples in 1550, was itself partly inspired by a treatise on military horsemanship written by the fourth-century B.C. Greek historian Xenophon. In the equestrian portrait the horse is far more than a prop. It is an emblem of social standing, breeding, and accomplishment.

Papal and ecclesiastical portraits relied to no less a degree on fixed formulas. Melozzo da Forlì's detached fresco from the papal library in the Vatican shows Pope Sixtus IV nominating the humanist Platina, who kneels before him, as prefect. The pope is shown in strict profile, seated, while Platina and Sixtus's handsome nephew Cardinal Giuliano della Rovere (the future Julius II, patron of Raphael and Michelangelo) assume less formal poses. The fictive pilasters framing the scene are decorated with branches of oak, the della Rovere family emblem. Raphael may not have used such obvious formulas to draw distinctions of status, but his portrait of the Medicean Pope Leo X with Cardinals Giulio de'Medici and Luigi de'Rossi (Galleria degli Uffizi, Florence) is just as powerful a statement on relative importance. An imposing chair and table with writing or reading implements became almost as indispensable to high-ranking ecclesiastics as did their brilliant red garb and dignified bearing.

Those who were neither rulers nor popes or cardinals might be shown more relaxed and in a more intimate setting, but if they occupied a position of standing, some allusion to it was invariably made. In Piero di Cosimo's portrait of the architect Giuliano da Sangallo, the sitter is shown before a landscape, as in contemporary Flemish portraits (which Piero doubtless knew), and behind a parapet on which are placed a pen and a compass used for drafting plans. Giuliano commissioned from Piero di Cosmo a companion picture of his father, in which the landscape background is a continuation of the one shown in his own portrait, but a sheet of music is substituted for the architect's instruments.

Giovanni Battista Moroni's beautiful portrait of Giovanni Bressani, painted in 1562, shows the poet and humanist in his study, the table piled with books and littered with letters and writings. Bressani is, indeed, shown as though interrupted in the act of writing, thereby at once alluding to his occupation and endowing the portrait with a quality of spontaneity. Bressani evidently entertained doubts about the effectiveness of prevailing portrait conventions, for the inscription on the piece of paper that projects over the edge of the table declares: "This painting is a good representation of my body, but my writings represent my soul."

Moroni was one of the few sixteenth-century painters who specialized in portraiture. Even if we lacked the identifying inscription on his depiction of Lucrezia Agliardi Vertova, the noble-born foundress of the Carmelite convent of Sant'Anna at Albino, near the Lombard city of Bergamo, the sitter's devout, if somewhat stern, character would be apparent. Nonetheless, Moroni saw fit to supply her with a prayer book.

In the eighteenth century a very different kind of portrait became popular: the well-to-do tourist taking in the sights and culture of Italy. No one ran a more popular studio for such figures than Pompeo Batoni, whose depictions of English travelers and aristocrats employ fragments of ancient architecture and sculpture to certify the sitter's interests and status. Rhetorical though these pictures may be, the sitters look no less ridiculous than many modern-day travelers posing before some celebrated landmark.

Titian (1488/89–1576)
Portrait of Charles V, 1548
Oil on canvas, 130⅝ x 109⅞" (332 x 279 cm)
Museo del Prado, Madrid

OPPOSITE:
Domenico Ghirlandaio (1449–1494)
The Approval of the Franciscan Rule, (detail), 1485
Fresco
Santa Trinita, Florence

Pisanello (before 1395–1455)
Lionello d'Este, 1441
Tempera on wood, 11 x 7½" (28 x 19 cm)
Accademia Carrara, Bergamo

OPPOSITE:
Jacopo Pontormo (1494–1556)
Cosimo il Vecchio de'Medici, ca. 1518–19
Oil on wood, 33⅞ x 25½" (86 x 65 cm)
Galleria degli Uffizi, Florence

203

Pompeo Batoni (1708–1787)
Edward Howard with His Dog Leaning against a
Parapet Overlooking the Roman Campagna, 1764–66
Oil on canvas, 54¾ x 39⅞" (139 x 101.5 cm)
Victoria and Albert Museum, London

OPPOSITE:
Melozzo da Forlì (1438–1494)
Sixtus IV Appointing Platina, 1474–77
Fresco, transferred to canvas
Pinacoteca Vaticana, Vatican

Agnolo Bronzino (1503–1572)
The Poet Laura Battiferri, ca. 1555–60
Oil on wood, 32⅝ x 23⅝" (83 x 60 cm)
Palazzo Vecchio, Florence

Giovanni Battista Moroni (1520–1578)
Abbess Lucrezia Agliardi Vertova, 1557
Oil on canvas, 35½ x 26⅜" (90.2 x 67 cm)
The Metropolitan Museum of Art, New York
Bequest of Theodore M. Davis, 1915
Theodore M. Davis Collection

OPPOSITE:
Giovanni Battista Moroni (1520–1578)
Portrait of Giovanni Bressani, 1562
Oil on canvas, 45¾ x 35" (116.2 x 88.8 cm)
National Gallery of Scotland, Edinburgh

18.
Dressing Up

Allegorical portraits in the 15ᵗʰ–18ᵗʰ centuries

In the days before inexpensive, portable cameras, it was common not only to commission formal, photo-graphic portraits requiring a sitting against a studio backdrop with chosen props and careful lighting—in imitation of painted portraits—but to record casual trips or outings to the fair or the beach with humor-ous snapshots showing the "sitter" poking his or her head through a hole in a painted scene, possibly of a muscle man with an admiring sex queen or a clown with his trained dog, or some such tableau. It is easy to forget that this simple amusement is the offspring of a wholly serious type of portraiture, whereby women of standing might be shown in the guise of the goddess Diana or a shepherdess, and men as Mars.

When, in 1802, the great neoclassical sculptor Antonio Canova was commissioned to create a work celebrating the achievements of Napoleon, he decided upon a statue that would flatter the general by show-ing him as a colossal nude imperator. This meant endowing the short, physically unattractive Corsican with the well-developed body of an athlete and displaying to full view his anatomy. In the sixteenth century Francis I of France was shown in an even more ridiculous, more complicated, and in the end more pro-grammatic guise. In one miniature the king's helmeted head is shown grafted onto the lithe limbs of a woman's body. With one armor-clad arm he raises a sword, while with the other he cradles the caduceus of Mercury. He has a quiver of arrows slung over his shoulder and on his delicate feet are winged sandals. To a casual viewer the portrait might be thought a political satire, but a rhymed verse appearing below this ludi-crous composite image explains: "Francis in war is a furious Mars, in peace Minerva, in the hunt Diana, in eloquence Mercury, and in love a true Cupid, full of grace." This astonishing accumulation of attributes concludes with: "O France, what a happy honor is the face of your great king who surpasses Nature, for in honoring him you serve at the same time Minerva, Mars, Diana, Cupid, and Mercury." No other portrait underscores so powerfully both the literary slant of these obsequiously flattering works and the seriousness with which they were offered up to an admiring audience (chief among whom was the sitter himself!).

In Italy, one of the earliest such portraits occurs in the center panel of an altarpiece begun by Masaccio in 1427/28 and completed following his death by his erstwhile partner Masolino. The picture records the fourth-century foundation of Santa Maria Maggiore in Rome following a miraculous summer snowfall that outlined the ground plan of the basilica. Pope Liberius is shown marking out the perimeter of the church with a hoe, assisted by the Patrician John. The altarpiece was commissioned by Pope Martin V, who had himself portrayed in the guise of his fourth-century predecessor together with Emperor Sigismund as the Patrician John. Martin had spearheaded a program of restoration for the churches of Rome, and to some extent the altarpiece commemorated this activity as well as his own dynastic preten-sions. We may shudder at the idea of a living president casting himself as George Washington, but no one seems to have thought less of Martin for usurping the role of an earlier pope. When Michelangelo viewed the work in the sixteenth century, he admired the lifelike quality the portraits conferred on the story. During the fifteenth century this sort of disguised portraiture became widespread. The Medici had them-selves portrayed in the retinue of the Magi in Benozzo Gozzoli's celebrated frescoes decorating the walls of their family chapel in the Medici Palace, and in the 1470s the Florentine money broker Giovanni del Lama sought to ingratiate himself with the Medici by having Botticelli show Cosimo il Vecchio as the old Magus, kneeling at the feet of the Virgin and Child, in a small altarpiece now in the Uffizi.

This type of disguised or "dressed-up" likeness was also adopted for individual portraits. In 1515 Giovanni Bellini showed a brother of the Dominican convent of Santi Giovanni e Paolo, Venice, in the guise of the thirteenth-century founder of the order, Saint Dominic (the sitter's name, Fra Teodoro da

Urbino, is recorded on an old inscription on the painting; National Gallery, London). This seems to have become a fashionable practice in the convent, for according to an account book, in 1548 Lorenzo Lotto showed another monk, Fra Zoan Andrea, in the guise of Saint Peter Martyr, presumably with the knife by which the saint was killed wedged into his skull. Carlo Dolci's seventeenth-century portrait of Claudia Felicita de'Medici as the fifth-century Roman empress Galla Placidia, who had married Alaric the Goth following the sack of Rome in 410 and was later an uncompromising Catholic and the builder of several famous churches in Ravenna (see chapter 3), is one of the most remarkable of these works.

Duke Cosimo I de'Medici had himself portrayed by Bronzino as a naked Orpheus charming the three-headed guardian of Hades, Cerberus, in a repellently erotic portrait, now in the Philadelphia Museum of Art, that was conceivably intended as an engagement gift for his future wife, Eleonora of Toledo, and the Genoese Andrea Doria, one of the greatest admirals of his age, adopted Neptune as his namesake. A statue of Doria in the guise of the sea god was commissioned from the Florentine Baccio Bandinelli, and an allegorical bronze plaquette showing Neptune urging the admiral on to greatness was made by Leone Leoni. The most astonishing of these images is unquestionably that by Bronzino, in which Doria's resolute head sits atop the muscular, assertively nude body of Neptune holding a trident. To anyone who imagines that societal conventions are of little importance to an understanding of the art of the past, these works by Bronzino are an abrupt refutation.

Equally revealing is the allegorical meaning that was applied to the Jewish heroine Judith, who rescued her people by decapitating the Assyrian general Holofernes. In the seventeenth century Cristofano Allori gave Judith the features of his lover, known as La Mazzafirra, and Judith's servant those of his lover's mother, while Holofernes' head bears his own likeness, reduced to misery by the trials of his mistress. It took only a change of story to convert the allegorized relationship into a homoerotic one: Caravaggio's painting of *David with the Head of Goliath* (Galleria Borghese, Rome) shows the painter's severed head held by his boy-lover Cecco. These biographical embellishments seem actually to have given the works in question added interest and luster for collectors.

Artemesia Gentileschi's depiction of herself as a personification of painting may seem conventional by comparison, but not so Salvator Rosa's *Self-Portrait as a Stoic Philosopher,* in which the painter makes a learned allusion to his perseverance in the face of hardships by showing himself crowned with cypress (an emblem of mourning), writing the Greek words for "Behold, whither, when." The picture was given to his good friend and moral philosopher Giovanni Battista Ricciardi.

Allegory attained a sort of peak in the self-congratulatory portrait the seventeenth-century castrato (male soprano) Marc'Antonio Pasqualini commissioned about 1640 from the Roman painter Andrea Sacchi. Marc'Antonio is depicted in the stage costume of a shepherd, wearing a bacchic leopard skin, accompanying a vocal performance on a keyed harp (a clavicytherium). The god Apollo crowns him with a wreath of laurel in honor of his achievement while in the background Marsyas, who had unsuccessfully challenged Apollo to a musical contest, is shown bound to a tree awaiting his punishment. The compliment is that Marc'Antonio—a favorite of the Barberini family—had accomplished what Marsyas had not been able to. Sacchi's biographer Giovanni Pietro Bellori described the picture as "not a simple portrait but a most beautiful conceit." To him, the artificiality constituted part of the picture's attraction. Today, when flattery is held in suspicion, it is almost impossible to fully appreciate these images, which are perhaps best approached as works of art and artifice rather than as portraits.

Masolino (1383–1440)
Founding of Santa Maria Maggiore Showing Pope Martin V in the Guise of Pope Liberius, ca. 1428
Tempera and gold on wood
56¾ x 30" (144 x 76 cm)
Museo Nazionale di Capodimonte, Naples

Carlo Dolci (1616–1686)
Claudia Felicita as Galla Placidia, 1672–75
Oil on canvas, 35 x 27½" (89 x 70 cm)
Galleria degli Uffizi, Florence

PAGE 212:
Agnolo Bronzino (1503–1572)
Andrea Doria, ca. 1540–45
Oil on canvas, 45¼ x 20⅞" (115 x 53 cm)
Pinacoteca di Brera, Milan

PAGE 213:
Andrea Sacchi (1599/1600–1655)
Marc'Antonio Pasqualini Crowned by Apollo, ca. 1640
Oil on canvas, 96 x 76½" (243.8 x 194.3 cm)
The Metropolitan Museum of Art, New York
Purchase, Enid A. Haupt Gift, Gwynne Andrews
Fund, and Purchase, 1871, by exchange, 1981

Artemisia Gentileschi (1593–1651/53)
Self-Portrait as an Allegory of Painting, 1630
Oil on canvas, 38 x 29" (96.5 x 73.7 cm)
Royal Collection, St. James's Palace, London

OPPOSITE:
Salvator Rosa (1615–1673)
Self-Portrait as a Stoic Philosopher, ca. 1656–57
Oil on canvas, 39 x 31¼" (99.1 x 79.4 cm)
The Metropolitan Museum of Art, New York
Bequest of Mary L. Harrison, 1921

19.
A Society of Men

Patriarchal portraits in the 15ᵗʰ–18ᵗʰ centuries

Portraiture as a means of investigating individual character and personality occurred in male portraits before it did in female ones and in portraits of well-to-do burghers rather than those of princes or aristocrats. That this is so is due not only to the obvious circumstance that most painters were men of similar, middle-class background, but to the fact that the success of merchants and bankers depended entirely on what we might call a sense of realism coupled with mental agility: the ability to size up a situation and outmaneuver a rival. Theirs was a game of wits, and it is no accident that Florence produced a distinguished line of chroniclers and historians, whose aim it was to record and explain significant events of the past, and also an unparalleled quantity of private diaries kept by citizens of frequently relatively modest means (over a hundred survive in the Florentine archives alone). On the whole, these are not works of introspection but of action, and it is the exterior aspect rather than the interior life of sitters that most interested Florentine painters and patrons. Typically, in his autobiography (in itself a sign of renewed interest in the individual) the humanist Pope Pius II, who was Sienese by birth, noted "the quick wits of the citizens [of Florence], though they excel most in trade, which philosophers think sordid. They seem too bent on making money . . . ."

Andrea del Castagno's *Portrait of a Man* shows one such person. His proud bearing, alert but guarded expression, and the firm resolve evident in the way his right hand grasps his cloak read like a catalogue of Florentine traits. With his intense gaze he seems to fix the viewer, already calculating our potential as a rival in business. This is perhaps the earliest surviving Italian portrait to break with the profile format, with its limited prospect of character analysis, and adopt the three-quarter view already familiar in Flemish painting. However, in characteristic fashion, the solid, assertive forms of Castagno's portrait are based on the study of sculptural busts rather than Flemish painting, and they epitomize the Florentine interest in the material aspect of the sitter and the world he lives in.

A generation later Domenico Ghirlandaio produced his sentimental portrait of an old man suffering from rhinophyma embracing his grandson. We know from a preparatory drawing that survives in Stockholm that the old man was dead when Ghirlandaio was commissioned to paint the picture, which was evidently meant to affirm a dynastic link between the deceased and his grandson and heir. To convey this, Ghirlandaio seized upon a conventional idea of a grandchild's fondness for his aging grandfather, actually playing down the deformation of the nose. It is the dynastic theme that explains the otherwise unusual double-portrait format.

A more truly introspective portrait emerged first in northern Europe, in Flanders, at the hands of Jan van Eyck, and made its appearance in Italy in the work of Antonello da Messina, who had direct knowledge of Flemish portraiture in Naples and in Venice, where he traveled in 1475 (see chapter 9). Antonello's portraits are the opposite of those of Castagno. Completely omitting the heavy drapery and hand by which Castagno communicated the impression of a man of action, Antonello focused exclusively on the face as a record of mental alertness, mapping out the wrinkles around the mouth and eyes and the set of the jaw with the care of a cartographer reconstructing the lay of the land. It is tempting to interpret the eyes of Antonello's portrait as the proverbial window of the soul, but in fact his sitter's thoughts are abstract and private: it is the presence rather the character of an inner life he evokes.

This reticence opened up somewhat in the sixteenth century, but one should not confuse the appearance of intimacy and informality with revelation of character. Rather, means were found to increase the allusive range and richness of portraiture without an undue invasion of privacy. No one was more skilled at this sort of virtuoso performance by which character is at once asserted and withheld than Bronzino, whose portraits of high-born Florentines are among the most complex and wonderful social masks ever created (see chapters 17 and 18).

It was the view of the great critic of Italian art Bernard Berenson that among the first artists to exhibit "a consciousness of self, a being aware at every moment of what is going on within one's heart and mind" was the Venetian contemporary of Titian, Lorenzo Lotto. Whereas "Titian never painted a single figure that does not have the look and bearing rank and circumstances require . . . Lotto would put the question, What sort of a person are you? How do you take life? Lotto was, in fact, the first Italian painter who was sensitive to the varying states of the human soul." Lotto appears to have been something of a nonconformist. He had a circle of protestant-leaning friends and never entered into the mainstream of Venetian life (eventually, he moved to the Marches). Yet to no less a degree than his fellow Venetian artists he preferred to codify his most personal observations in emblems that sometimes serve to unlock the secrets of the personality or the motives of his sitters. Opinion had it that what could be understood by anyone was not worth knowing and that, conversely, Truth was profaned if presented in common or plain terms. The elaborate hieroglyphs beloved by Lotto were intended to reveal otherwise hidden truths while maintaining a quality of mystery.

His portrait in the Accademia in Venice of a young man in his study casually flipping through the pages of a thick treatise may seem a remarkably intimate depiction in which the sitter appears to have been caught unaware, but this is a fiction. The hunting horn and lute that hang from a cornice refer to his culture and pastimes, while before him lie an opened letter, scattered rose petals, a ring, and an inquisitive lizard. The rose petals and the ring probably allude to a trial of love, possibly conveyed by the letter, and the lizard may signify the jealousy that is at the center of the problem. Is it to console or distract himself that this pensive youth has diffidently turned to the treatise in front of him? Perhaps only in the recent autobiographical work of Jasper Johns has an artist disguised his meaning so eloquently behind a rebus of emblems, each carrying its own association.

To appreciate the complexity of Lotto's portraits, we have only to compare them with a work like the alluring portrayal of a child proudly displaying his handiwork by Lotto's Veronese contemporary Francesco Caroto, deceptively like a spontaneous snapshot, or Domenichino's early seventeenth-century depiction of the amateur art critic Giovanni Battista Agucchi (City Art Gallery, York), which has the appearance of a straightforward testimony to a longstanding friendship. Serodine's portrait of an old man seated behind a table, evidently his father, has the unsettling character of a personal confession of a complex if loving relationship. In looking at these works it is well to remember that the sixteenth century witnessed new advances in the understanding of human character, both in the area of biography—one thinks of the autobiography of Michel de Montaigne—and in religion, whether one thinks of Martin Luther or Saint Teresa of Avila. The founder of the Jesuits, Ignatius Loyola, was quick to use these insights in the creation of a program of controlled thought leading to contrition and spiritual renewal (*The Spiritual Exercises*). Although in the popular imagination Jesuit art has become synonymous with rhetorical display and pomposity, it may not be accidental that one of the most arresting seventeenth-century portraits is that by the Neapolitan painter Jusepe de Ribera of an unknown Jesuit priest—judging from the exotic lion, he was possibly a missionary to one of those areas of the globe the Jesuits were so quick to evangelize. In looking at these portraits we may feel that the distance between sixteenth- and seventeenth-century sensibilities and our own is not so very great, but the fact is that seventeenth-century society was hierarchical, and each of these portraits comments on the status of the sitter as well as on his character.

Perhaps nowhere is the development of Italian portraiture so well encapsulated as in a series of self-revealing or self-deceiving self-portraits. These range from the brilliant conceit of the young Parmigianino, who chose to view his hypersensitive features reflected in the distorting surface of a convex mirror (in a fashion typical of the sophistication of Mannerist art he paints his reflected "appearance" rather than his "reality"); to the unembellished depiction by Annibale Carracci of himself at work in his studio (a sort of manifesto of the artist's belief in Nature as the mother of art); to that encomium of social superiority created by the Neapolitan Francesco Solimena (Museo Nazionale di San Martino, Naples), in which the artist, dressed like an academician rather than a painter, is ensconced in luxury before his easel, his face turned toward the viewer with an expression of withering arrogance. It is Solimena's self-portrait that reminds us how distant the artist's concerns were from those of our own era.

Domenico Ghirlandaio (1449–1494)
Old Man and His Grandson, ca. 1480
Tempera on wood, 24⅜ x 18⅛" (62.7 x 46.3 cm)
Musée du Louvre, Paris

Andrea del Castagno (1417/19–1457)
Portrait of a Man, ca. 1450
Tempera on wood, 21¼ x 15⅞" (54 x 40.5 cm)
National Gallery of Art, Washington
Andrew W. Mellon Collection

Parmigianino (1503–1540)
Self-Portrait, 1524
Oil on wood, diameter 9⅝" (24.4 cm)
Kunsthistorisches Museum, Vienna

Francesco Caroto (1480–1555)
Portrait of a Boy, ca. 1520–25
Oil on wood, 14½ x 11⅜" (37 x 29 cm)
Museo di Castelvecchio, Verona

221

Lorenzo Lotto (ca. 1480–1556)
Portrait of a Gentleman, ca. 1528
Oil on canvas, 38½ x 43¾" (98 x 111 cm)
Accademia, Venice

OPPOSITE:
Annibale Carracci (1560–1609)
Self-Portrait, ca. 1585
Oil on canvas, 23⅝ x 18⅞" (60 x 48 cm)
Pinacoteca di Brera, Milan

222

223

Jusepe de Ribera (1591–1652)
Portrait of a Jesuit, 1638
Oil on canvas, 76¾ x 43⅜"
(195 x 110 cm)
Museo Poldi Pezzoli, Milan

225

20.
The Second Sex

Portraits of women in the 15ᵗʰ–18ᵗʰ centuries

Among the most persistent images of Italy is that of a quintessentially patriarchal society—a world in which men reign supreme. Yet the reverse side of this image—of the weak male dominated by the omnipresent mother—figures no less prominently in contemporary mythology. The relative merits of men and women were already the subject of dispute in the Renaissance, when Castiglione devoted a number of pages to it in his book *The Courtier.* On the one hand, there was the conventional view of Gaspare Pallavicino to the effect that "woman are imperfect creatures and therefore of less dignity than men and incapable of practicing the virtues practiced by men . . .; when a woman is born this is a mistake or defect, and contrary to Nature's wishes." On the other hand, there was the more benign opinion of Giuliano de'Medici that "being weaker in body women are abler in mind and more capable of speculative thought than men. . . . I say that if you will consider the operation of Nature, you will find that she produces women the way they are not by chance but adapted to the necessary end; for although she makes them gentle in body and placid in spirit, and with many other qualities opposite to those of men, yet the attribute of the one and the other tend towards the same beneficial end." What both men agreed upon, more or less, were the qualities to be prized in a woman. Among these were "a certain soft and delicate tenderness. . . . [She should be] well mannered, clever, and prudent; to be neither envious or evil tongued, nor vain, contentious, or clumsy." And, of course, a woman should be faithful.

Marriage was a serious matter in the Renaissance (and, indeed, in Catholic Europe down to the twentieth century). As a means of alliance between two families, of attaining social prominence or wealth, it was entered into with the care of a business proposition, and the conventions governing its realization were both intricate and practical, in full recognition of the worth of the enterprise. Love, of course, was a secondary concern.

It is as a proud possession that Angiola di Bernardo Sapiti is shown in Filippo Lippi's *Portrait of a Man and a Woman at a Casement,* painted about 1436 in commemoration of her marriage to Lorenzo Scolari. Dressed in the latest French fashion, her head adorned with a velvet, pearl-encrusted hat (known as a *sella*), her underdress composed of a dark blue brocade, her overdress of a belted, fur-lined red velvet, Angiola is decked out in all her richness. Set, like a precious stone, in a boxlike room opened at the back by a window, she exhibits on her sleeve an embroidered inscription, *Lealtà* (faithfulness). Her husband has been inserted as the proud owner of this remarkable woman, his hands resting on a coat of arms that makes the identification of the sitters possible.

At the opposite end of the spectrum is Leonardo da Vinci's compelling portrait of the wife of Francesco del Giocondo, Lisa Gherardini, the person we know as Mona (that is, madonna or milady) Lisa and whom the French and Italians call *La Gioconda.* Leonardo was evidently commissioned to paint her portrait in Florence in 1503, but there is no evidence that it was ever delivered. Rather, Leonardo kept the picture for himself, his fertile mind working its transforming power on the raw material of nature. The picture, which seems first to turn up in the inventory of a pupil and was then purchased for the French royal collection, is a portrait only insofar as its genesis is concerned. Clearly, at some point Lisa Gherardini became a muselike figure for Leonardo. Although popular imagination has identified the sitter's smile as the picture's most haunting feature, it is the conjunction of the real and the ideal that explains the mysterious allure this aloof creature has exerted ever since Leonardo's day.

Resemblance was a foremost concern in male portraits. Not so in female ones, where as often as not conformity to an ideal of beauty imposed a certain uniformity. It is not uncommon to come away from fifteenth-century female portraits with the uneasy feeling that the women belonged one and all to the same family. When, in 1493 Isabella d'Este asked her court artist Andrea Mantegna to paint her likeness, he seems to have gone about the task in his habitual, unflattering manner. Offended at the results, Isabella rejected the portrait and hired a less talented artist whose great virtue was that his portraits were so bland as to provoke no disappointment. Isabella's favorite portrait was another one she never sat to at all: she found that it improved upon what Nature had granted her. Painted by the Bolognese Francesco Francia, this portrait was sent to Titian in 1534–36 to paint an ideal likeness of Isabella as a young woman. Titian was an experienced courtier, and when his portrait of Isabella was sent to her, she was delighted, even if she had to confess that she had probably never been this beautiful. What Titian had captured was Isabella's idea of herself—a composite of her face and her much praised cultural accomplishments—and it would be a gross misunderstanding to expect of this beautiful portrait a modern study in feminine psychology.

Despite the fact that numerous female portraits of an extraordinary probing character survive from the seventeenth and eighteenth centuries—two remarkable ones are Guido Reni's sensitive *Portrait of a Widow* (traditionally identified as his mother), and Giacomo Ceruti's homely *Girl with a Fan*—it might be maintained that the male artists who depicted female sitters imposed on them their own preconceptions about women in general. For this reason, special interest attaches to the handful of self-portraits by women artists. That by the Cremonese Sofonisba Anguissola, the most talented of five sister-painters is particularly compelling. Sofonisba was much celebrated as a female artist. Invited to the court of Philip II of Spain in 1559, she later married a Sicilian knight and, after his death, a Genoese knight. Her portraits are products of the aristocratic circles in which she moved and reveal the intelligence and sophistication that made her drawings admired even by the hypercritical Michelangelo. Rosalba Carriera, who lived two centuries later, was a different personality altogether. Her career began humbly as a lace maker, but when the market for lace slumped, she took up painting snuffboxes and gradually worked up to portraiture. She became a member of the Accademia di San Luca in Rome in 1705 and by 1720 was so well known in international circles that her arrival in Paris was widely feted. She never married, remaining committed to her profession to the end, her work interrupted only by letter writing and music making. Late in her life, blindness put an end to her splendid career. Her self-portrait in the Accademia, Venice, shows her toward the end of her life, her lips firm but sensitive, her critical gaze averted. Neither of these works is without social pretension—typically, Sofonisba has shown herself at a spinet and Rosalba has alluded to her accomplishments by the laurels adorning her gray hair—but they carry a personal message of professional achievement that sets them apart from more conventional portraits.

PAGE 228:
Filippo Lippi (1406–1469)
Portrait of a Man and a Woman at a Casement, ca. 1436
Tempera on wood, 25 ¼ x 16 ½"
(64.1 x 41.9 cm)
The Metropolitan Museum of Art, New York
Gift of Henry G. Marquand, 1889
Marquand Collection

PAGE 229:
Leonardo da Vinci (1452–1519)
Mona Lisa, ca. 1503–5
Oil on wood, 30 ¼ x 20 ⅞"
(77 x 53 cm)
Musée du Louvre, Paris

229

230

OPPOSITE:
Giacomo Ceruti (1698–1767)
Girl with a Fan, ca. 1740
Oil on canvas, 25 ⅝ x 23 ¼" (65 x 59 cm)
Accademia Carrara, Bergamo

Sofonisba Anguissola (1532/33–1625)
Self-Portrait at a Spinet, ca. 1560
Oil on canvas, 22 x 19" (56 x 48 cm)
Museo Nazionale di Capodimonte, Naples

Guido Reni (1575–1642)
Portrait of a Widow (the Artist's Mother?), ca. 1630
Oil on canvas, 25¼ x 21⅝" (64 x 55 cm)
Pinacoteca Nazionale, Bologna

Rosalba Carriera (1675–1757)
Self-Portrait, ca. 1750
Pastel on paper, 12¼ x 9⅞" (31 x 25 cm)
Accademia, Venice

233

21.
Ideal Women

Pinups in the 15th–18th centuries

As every student of Italian literature knows, Dante had his Beatrice and Petrarch, his Laura. Dante was nine when he met the girl who was eventually to guide him to his heavenly vision in the *Divine Comedy*, but even at that tender age she seemed to him "so praiseworthy and noble that indeed the words of the poet Homer might have said of her: 'She did not seem the daughter of a mortal man, but of a god.'" For Petrarch too, Laura was far more than a pretty woman: she was the source of a perfect, because unconsummated, love, the delectation of which extended beyond her earthly existence. He first saw her on April 6, 1327, in the church of Saint Clare in Avignon; she died twenty-one years later, on precisely the same day: "The eyes of which I so warmly spoke, and the arms, the hand, the feet, and the face that separated me from myself, and marked me out from other people; the waving hair of pure shining gold, and the flashing of her angelic smile that used to make a paradise on earth are little more than dust, feeling nothing."

Petrarch had the portrait of his beloved Laura painted by Simone Martini. It must have been an ideal likeness, epitomizing her perfect traits, for Petrarch devoted two poems to it, in one of which he declared, "Certainly my Simone was in Paradise where that sweet lady has gone; there he saw her and drew her likeness to give credence here below to her beautiful face."

Simone's painting has long since disappeared, but in the early sixteenth century Giorgione, who was closely associated with Pietro Bembo, a champion of Petrarchan verse, painted a picture that survives showing a beautiful woman against a branch of laurel, an allusion to Laura's name (Kunsthistorisches Museum, Vienna). The model, who modestly exposes a breast, may have been a professional courtesan, but that is not its point. In *The Courtier,* Bembo is made to declare, "Love is simply a certain longing to possess beauty . . . and we shall argue that this beauty is an influx of the divine goodness which, like the light of the sun, is shed over all created things, but especially . . . when it discovers and informs a countenance which is well proportioned and composed of a certain joyous harmony of various colors enhanced by light and shadow and by symmetry and clear definition." Giorgione's picture stands at the head of a long line of paintings that take as their point of departure Petrarch's poems describing his beloved and that have as their object the exaltation of beauty.

In some of these pictures of idealized women the depicted beauty was inspired by a real person. This is, for example, the case with Raphael's portrait of his mistress, the Fornarina (whose amorous demands, according to Vasari, precipitated Raphael's premature death). Her small chin, majestically arched brows, large, dark eyes, and delicately soft fingers pressing against her full, naked breast (a pose that derives from ancient statues of Venus covering her private parts) are all traits Bembo would have approved of, and as in Giorgione's painting, her ivory body is set against a dark background of laurel and myrtle (myrtle being a plant associated with Venus and love). On her arm she wears what might be described as a lover's bracelet: an embroidered ribbon with Raphael's name.

Parmigianino's painting of a young woman was also evidently inspired by a Roman courtesan who took her name, Antea, from the character of a popular epic poem. The uncertainty in identifying the sitter of this marvelous work derives from the fact that Parmigianino, like Raphael, has endowed his model— with whom he may or may not have had an amorous relationship—with traits derived from poetic convention: her long neck, small chin, large eyes, and elegant hands. He has, in other words, elevated her to an ideal realm. That similar features are found in his *Madonna of the Long Neck* (see chapter 11) only serves to underscore how pervasive this concern for an artificially perfected beauty was and how intertwined it became with notions of a divine emanation.

Palma Vecchio (ca. 1480–1528)
The Three Sisters, ca. 1520
Oil on canvas, 34⅝ x 48⅜"
(88 x 123 cm)
Gemäldegalerie Alte
Meister—Staatliche
Kunstsammlungen Dresden

PAGE 236:
Piero di Cosimo (1461/62–1521)
*Portrait of a Woman, called
Simonetta Vespucci*, ca. 1485–90
Oil on wood, 22½ x 16½"
(57 x 42 cm)
Musée Condé, Chantilly

PAGE 237:
Attributed to Bartolomeo Veneto
(active between 1502 and 1530)
Portrait of a Courtesan (?), ca. 1520–30
Oil on wood, 17⅛ x 13½"
(43.5 x 34.3 cm)
Städelsches Kunstinstitut, Frankfurt

In the same way, Piero di Cosimo's magical portrait of a maiden with a snake around her neck—is it an attribute of Cleopatra or Persephone, or a Neoplatonic conceit?—bears an old inscription identifying the sitter as Simonetta Vespucci, the mistress of Giuliano de'Medici and the inspiration for Poliziano's heroine in the *Giostra*.

Titian's contemporary Palma Vecchio specialized in this genre, but on a more earthly, base plane. His painting known as the *Three Sisters* shows what are quite obviously three courtesans whose similar appearance and blond hair (frequently achieved through bleaching or the use of a wig) and full, soft features could be had for the right price in sixteenth-century Venice. The pastoral landscape behind them emphasizes the degree to which poetic conventions have transformed the hard reality of prostitution into a romantic idyll. In other works, Palma provided his women with lutes—that potent accompaniment to love. Some of these courtesans became quite famous not only for their beauty but for their culture (Antea is an example), and Palma's pictures are part of this propaganda of purchased love. His paintings must have been collected and hung for private delectation: a sophisticated equivalent to modern pinups. Bartolomeo Veneto excelled in the same vein, though his pictures are less sensuously alluring. Curiously, the woman who is the subject of the haunting picture in Frankfurt attributed to him wears the veil of a bride and holds a carnation, a common symbol of engagement. Yet this can hardly be a marriage picture.

This genre, so closely allied to the popularity of images of a nude Venus reclining on a couch—the true nature of which Manet unmasked when he transformed Titian's celebrated *Venus of Urbino* into the prostitute *Olimpia*—retained its appeal through the seventeenth and eighteenth centuries. Even that realist Caravaggio gave a nod to it in his painting of the courtesan Phillis (formerly in Berlin; destroyed in World War II). In the eighteenth century Tiepolo painted his picture of a Venetian beauty, her hair adorned with flowers, a breast discreetly exposed, with that effective symbol of lust, an excited parrot (Ashmolean Museum, Oxford).

Interestingly, Giorgione, the artist who had done so much to popularize the genre, also created its nemesis: an old woman looking out of the picture while she calls attention to her withered appearance with a scroll inscribed *col tempo*, "with time." An old woman frequently accompanies a young prostitute in procuress scenes, both in Italian and in northern painting, but nowhere else is the transient nature of beauty "here below" made so poignantly real.

237

Parmigianino (1503–1540)
Antea, ca. 1535–37
Oil on canvas, 53¼ x 34⅝" (135 x 88 cm)
Museo Nazionale di Capodimonte, Naples

Raphael (1483–1520)
The Fornarina, ca. 1517
Oil on wood, 33½ x 23⅝" (85 x 60 cm)
Galleria Borghese, Rome

Giorgione (1476/77–1510)
The Old Woman (Col Tempo), ca. 1508–10
Oil on canvas, 26¾ x 23¼" (68 x 59 cm)
Accademia, Venice

22.
Landscapes of the Imagination
Ideal landscape painting in the 16th–18th centuries

"Happy is the man who far from the cares of business, like the ancient generations of man, works his ancestral fields with his own oxen, free of all usury," wrote the ancient poet Vergil in the *Georgics*, one of the most admired paeans of country life ever written. It is a commonplace that an idealization of the country and an appreciation of the beauties of a pastoral landscape are the concomitant of urban life, and it is hardly surprising that a by-product of the mercantile societies of Renaissance Italy was the invention of landscape painting as an independent genre. This development was encouraged and shaped by the humanist interest in ancient literature: in Vergil's *Georgics,* Ovid's description of a lost golden age, Statius's *Silvae,* the letters of Pliny concerning his Tuscan villa, and Theocritus's portrayal of the life of the common people of Sicily in the *Idyls.*

It was in imitation of Roman villas that the Medici built their many retreats in the hills surrounding Florence, culminating in that extraordinary creation of Poggio a Caiano, with its pedimented portico and its great hall frescoed by Andrea del Sarto and Pontormo. And it was for Venetians seeking, "like the ancient generations of man," a farm retreat that Palladio designed his villas in the Veneto. "Let him who desires pomp and honor seek the squares, the temples and great buildings, pleasures, and treasure accompanied by a thousand hard thoughts and a thousand griefs. A green meadow filled with lovely flowers, a stream that washes the banks, a little bird that makes its plaint of love, these soothe our restlessness far better," wrote Lorenzo the Magnificent, pleasantly ensconced in one of his villas. Near Venice, an escape from the pressures of city life was provided by Caterina Cornaro, the deposed queen of Cyprus, who held her literary court gatherings at Asolo, in the gentle hills of the Veneto, not far from Giorgione's birthplace at Castelfranco. Giorgione and the poet Pietro Bembo were part of this pastoral salon, at which the main topic seems to have been love, to judge from Bembo's *Asolani* immortalizing the conversations.

Not surprisingly, Giorgione was the first to give visual form to this romanticized vision of the pastoral life. The picture, now in the Accademia, Venice, was seen by the collector-critic Marcantonio Michiel in the house of Gabriel Vendramin in 1530. Despite the fact that Michiel was an unusually well-informed connoisseur, he seems to have been baffled by the subject of the painting, which he described simply as "the small landscape with the storm ('tempesta'), the gipsy, and the soldier." Although many attempts have been made to push the matter further, all have run up against the fundamental novelty of the work, in which the action—or the lack of it—is secondary to the overall mood produced by the flash of lightning illuminating a river landscape with an old, battered wall and ancient ruins, whence the title of the work, the *Tempesta.* It is possible that Giorgione intended some sort of allegory, with allusions to fortitude (the broken columns in the middle ground), charity (the gypsy nursing her child), and fortune (the storm), but the real point of the picture is its poetic mood, not some hidden meaning. This is borne out by the fact that X rays show that in place of the soldier Giorgione originally intended to paint another female nude. The painting initiated the revival of idyllic landscapes populated with nymphs, shepherds, bathers, or city folk on an amorous outing with musical instruments: a rediscovered Arcadia such as the poet Sannazaro had described in his work by that name.

These are essentially escapist paintings in which the poetic tone was determined by an intense nostalgia for a simpler, mythic past seen through the eyes of ancient authors. Nowhere is this quality more deeply felt than in those paintings which combine the pleasure of a summer idyll with a reminder of the transience of life: in Titian's *Three Ages of Man* (National Gallery of Scotland, Edinburgh) or the painting of the same theme by his Ferrarese contemporary Dosso Dossi, in which the inexorable march of time is alluded to by the presence of two children spying on lovers and, in the background, two old men deep in conversation; or in those paintings by Poussin and Guercino in which shepherds happen upon a tomb, reminding them that even in Arcadia there is no escape from death. At other times, country pleasures are unspoiled by any reminder of mortality. This is the case with a small painting by Guercino (Museum Boymans-van Beuningen, Rotterdam) showing women bathing at a ruined fountain while, in the distance, a hunt goes on (is there an allusion to the story of Actaeon, who was transformed into a stag when discovered spying on Diana and her virgin nymphs?).

Another, related type of landscape—equally divorced from the world of the everyday—took as its point of departure a specific story from classical mythology. For Niccolò dell'Abate the rape of Proserpina by the god of the underworld—enacted in two episodes in the foreground and on the cliff at the right—was largely an excuse for depicting a fantastical landscape composed of ruined castles and rocky outcrops painted in shades of blue. The landscape was patently inspired by those of the Netherlandish painter Patinir and his school, which enjoyed enormous popularity in Venice and Ferrara. In this work a celebrated Greek myth is transposed by its setting into a chivalric tale in which the figures are caught up as in a ballet. The bizarre effect was intentional and had its counterpart in the contemporary literature of Ferrara, inspired in equal measure by French chivalric literature and ancient epics. Ironically, one of the masterpieces of that literary school, Torquato Tasso's *Jerusalem Delivered*, received a thoroughly classical treatment by the seventeenth-century painter Pier Francesco Mola, in his depiction of Erminia writing the name of her beloved on a tree while she watches her sheep. Rather than adopt the surreal landscape that so appealed to Niccolò dell'Abate's Mannerist fancy, Mola based his landscape on the Venetian pastoral vision of Giorgione and Titian, thereby revealing the inherent romanticism of both the literary and the artistic basis of these imaginary landscapes.

By the early sixteenth century, artists in Rome had seen ancient frescoes and were able to pattern their evocations of classical landscapes on real examples. No one came closer to imitating the impressionistic technique associated with Roman frescoes than Raphael's gifted pupil Polidoro da Caravaggio in his mural paintings in San Silvestro al Quirinale, Rome. The landscapes are unusual in that they decorate the walls of a chapel rather the interior of a villa, and their subject is religious, not secular. Yet as so often with these landscape paintings, subject seems secondary to the soaring hills, sheets of water, dense groves of trees, and ancient-style temples. What Polidoro achieved was the fusion of the brio that is the singular attraction of ancient landscape painting with that quality of expansiveness and structure we associate with the Renaissance. In turn, his work served as the point of departure for Annibale Carracci's noble landscapes in the Palazzo Doria Pamphili, painted as lunettes for a private chapel for the nephew of Pope Clement VIII (as with Polidoro's, the subjects were religious). These, in turn, were the basis of the classical visions of Domenichino, Poussin, and Claude Lorraine (although the latter two were Frenchmen, virtually the whole of their careers was spent in Rome, and their work is inseparable from Italian painting).

To a degree, even Guardi's fantastic landscapes, painted a century later, can be seen as an extension of this continued fascination with Roman fresco practice and imaginary landscapes. But his pictures are, at the same time, assertions of the imaginative faculty of the artist over and above the dictates of nature. The same is true of the untamed wilds of Alessandro Magnasco's landscape settings.

Nowhere do these various strands—the evocation of the lost, ruined world of antiquity and the exaltation of the artist's imagination—come into play so brilliantly as in the series of allegorical tombs commemorating the heroes of modern English history that were commissioned in the 1720s from a variety of Venetian and Bolognese painters by the playwright and one-time London theater manager Owen McSwiney. In Sebastiano and Marco Ricci's *Memorial to Admiral Sir Clowdisley Shovell*, architecture and landscape conspire to create a poetic vision for which there is no counterpart in the less literary-inspired, more pedestrian landscape paintings of later artists—at least before the arrival of de Chirico (see chapter 27).

Giorgione (1476/77–1510)
The Tempesta, ca. 1506–8
Oil on canvas, 26¾ x 23¾" (68 x 59 cm)
Accademia, Venice

Dosso Dossi (active by 1512, died 1542)
The Three Ages of Man, ca. 1520–24
Oil on canvas, 30½ x 44" (77.5 x 111.8 cm)
The Metropolitan Museum of Art, New York
Maria DeWitt Jesup Fund, 1926

OPPOSITE TOP:
Annibale Carracci (1560–1609)
The Flight into Egypt, ca. 1604
Oil on canvas, 48 x 90½" (122 x 230 cm)
Galleria Doria Pamphili, Rome

Niccolò dell'Abate (1509?–1571?)
Rape of Proserpina, ca. 1552–70
Oil on canvas, 77⅛ x 85" (196 x 216 cm)
Musée du Louvre, Paris

OPPOSITE BOTTOM:
Pier Francesco Mola (1612–1666)
Erminia and Her Flocks, ca. 1655–60
Oil on canvas, 28 x 37" (71 x 94 cm)
Musée du Louvre, Paris

244

Francesco Guardi (1712–1793)
Fantastic Landscape, 1760s
Oil on canvas, 61¼ x 74½" (155.5 x 189.2 cm)
The Metropolitan Museum of Art, New York
Gift of Julia A. Berwind, 1953

PAGE 248:
Donato Creti (1671–1749)
Astronomical Observation of Venus, 1711–12
Oil on canvas, 20¼ x 13¾" (51.5 x 35 cm)
Pinacoteca Vaticana, Vatican

PAGE 249:
Sebastiano (1659–1734) and Marco Ricci
(1676–1730)
Memorial to Admiral Sir Clowdisley Shovell, ca. 1725
Oil on canvas, 87½ x 62½" (222.3 x 158.8 cm)
National Gallery of Art, Washington
Samuel H. Kress Collection

23.
Landscapes of Fact

Topographical views in the 15th–18th centuries

In northern Europe, and especially in seventeenth-century Holland, there arose a type of landscape painting based less on a poetic conceit or nostalgia for the distant past than on an appreciation of the real—albeit imperfect—beauties of the surrounding countryside: a wooded path, a flat field dotted by drying linen, a chilly beach populated with fishmongers, a mountain stream. Such landscapes seem to have exerted relatively little appeal for Italian painters and collectors, though the backgrounds of fifteenth-century altarpieces—such as Pollaiuolo's *Martyrdom of Saint Sebastian*, Piero della Francesca's *Baptism of Christ*, and Giovanni Bellini's *Saint Francis* (see chapters 8 and 9)—demonstrate that a response to nature was in no way lacking. In Italy, factual landscapes of this sort were the exception, not the rule. When, however, it came to recording the appearance of cities, a different mentality prevailed.

Topographical landscape painting in Italy is linked to three factors: the urge to document historical events, the invention of perspective, and the advent of tourism. In 1331 Simone Martini was paid by the commune of Siena for the expenses he had incurred traveling to southern Tuscany to take topographical views of the recently conquered castles at Arcidosso and Castel del Piano. He was to add depictions of these to the cycle of frescoes in the Palazzo Pubblico showing the outposts of the Sienese state (see chapter 6). A similar commemorative function underlies one of the early topographical depictions of Florence, a view of the Piazza della Signoria taken on the occasion of the burning of Savonarola in 1498. Among the earliest depictions of Venice are those in which the city's squares and canals appear as the backdrop for religious ceremonies (see chapter 9). Carpaccio's panoramic view of the Basin of San Marco behind the symbolic lion of Saint Mark was painted in 1516 to adorn a state office (it comes from the treasurer's palace and bears the arms of five prominent families). The Doges' Palace is shown as viewed from the island of San Giorgio Maggiore, but the tower of the Arsenal, seen on the right, has been included for its military importance and is not visible from that spot.

Commemorative or documentary views such as these recur intermittently throughout Italian painting, from an anonymous fifteenth-century view of the Bay of Naples with the naval fleet of Alfonso V returning from the liberation of the island of Ischia (Museo di Nazionale San Martino, Naples) to Domenico Gargiulo's depiction of the city during an eruption of Vesuvius in 1631 or his grisly view of the Piazza Mercatello at the height of the plague in 1656, painted not for the Neapolitan state but for a private collector, Antonio Piscicelli, who seems to have had a particular interest in documenting the contemporary history of his city.

In Rome, the Barberini commissioned works from their resident artist, Andrea Sacchi, and the perspective specialist Filippo Gagliardi of festivities they financed: the centenary celebrations at Il Gesù and a lavish spectacle presented in Piazza Navona on February 25, 1634 (Museo di Roma, Rome). Guardi carried out twelve canvases depicting the solemnities of the doge which fall into this same category. By contrast, a canvas by Antonio Joli showing the young King Ferdinand and his retinue outside the palace of Capodimonte seems to a large extent an excuse for depicting Naples and its incomparable bay drenched in the light of the setting sun (Museo Nazionale di Capodimonte, Naples).

The urge to document important events would have assured the making of the occasional topographical view, but what raised depictions of the urban landscape to an art was the invention of perspective by Filippo Brunelleschi in the years around 1420. Brunelleschi demonstrated the principles of one-point or vanishing point perspective on two oblong panels, one of which showed the baptistery of Florence as viewed from the cathedral opposite, and the other, the Piazza della Signoria. What differentiated these views from earlier depictions of an identifiable building or castle, such as those by Simone Martini or the Lorenzetti (see chapter 6), was their cartographic accuracy, which seemed to raise the topographical view to the status of a science. Imaginary or ideal city views soon achieved the status of demonstration pieces. They adorned chests, choir stalls, and sacristy cupboards, where they were carried out in pieces of different colored wood (intarsia), and they became the setting, par excellence, of narrative subjects. Whether it was Filippino Lippi's depiction of the story of the biblical heroine Esther (Musée du Louvre, Paris, and Musée Condé, Chantilly), painted in the early 1480s, or Viviano Codazzi's *Massacre of the Innocents,* perhaps painted about 1660, the setting of choice was an urban landscape laid out according to the laws of perspective. Codazzi was a specialist in perspective, and as Sacchi and Gagliardi did in the views already mentioned, he entrusted the figures in his work to another artist: Filippo Lauri seems to have painted the figures in the *Massacre of the Innocents.* In this picture the setting, not the subject, was of primary importance.

The factor that altered the course of topographical painting was the advent of international tourism and the desire on the part of wealthy foreigners—especially the British—to return home with a souvenir of their travels. Then, as now, the two cities that figured highest on the list of stops were Venice, with its canals, and Rome, with its ancient ruins. These two cities, together with the Bay of Naples (which enraptured Brueghel when he visited the city in 1552), are the subjects of the majority of eighteenth-century views. In Venice, Luca Carlevaris was the first artist to devote himself to *vedute,* or view paintings, but it was Canaletto whose name became synonymous with it. His earliest documented works, from 1725, were painted for an Italian, Stefano Conti of Lucca, but already the following year he was working for the Irishman Owen McSwiney, who sold Canaletto's work directly to English collectors. British collectors were to be the primary source of Canaletto's income for the rest of his life. Indeed, he eventually moved temporarily to London, where he continued to produce views of Venice as well as of London and the surrounding country.

Canaletto also painted some views of Rome, the other major city tourists wanted pictures of. These were apparently done from drawings and do not record any direct response to the city, which he appears to have visited only once, in 1719–20; his series of five views of Rome date from 1742. The master of the Roman *veduta* was Giovanni Paolo Pannini. As with Canaletto, Pannini's views fall into two categories: truly topographical views that correspond more or less to what can actually be seen when standing at a given location, and *capricci*—fantasies in which the artist either combined famous sights into a composite postcard or freely invented views suggestive of the picturesque beauty of Venice, in Canaletto's case, or the grandeur of Rome, in Pannini's. The defect of both painters is that the intense demand for their work far exceeded their abilities to supply them single-handed. Both artists not only came to rely upon an active workshop, but they created shorthand techniques (sometimes erroneously described as proto-impressionistic) and an emphasis on the architectural elements, which could be laid in with a draftsman's instruments, over atmospheric unity. Fortunately, this is not the case with Canaletto's best work, such as his marvelously evocative early view of the Campo di Santi Giovanni e Paolo (Gemäldegalerie, Dresden) and that unsurpassed view of Venice in Boston, in which the quality of atmosphere is grasped to perfection and the city seems palpably real.

It was this sensitivity to atmosphere—all too rare in his own work—that Canaletto passed on to his nephew Belotto, who left Venice for the courts of Vienna, Dresden, Munich, and Warsaw in 1747 and, in consequence, has never enjoyed the celebrity of Canaletto. Yet, as his views of Verona and of the village of Gazzada demonstrate, he had a more acute eye than his uncle for variations of light and atmosphere, and he had a real feeling for the lives of ordinary people. He was, perhaps, the greatest topographical painter of the eighteenth century. So keen was his feeling for place that it is not uncommon when standing in front of his thirteen views of Vienna and the imperial castles, carried out for the empress Maria Teresa between 1758 and 1761 (Kunsthistorisches Museum, Vienna), to feel that one is in the presence of a social commentator of the highest order and not a mere painter of *vedute.*

252

Domenico Gargiulo (Micco Spadaro) (1609–1675)
Piazza Mercatello, Naples, during the Plague of 1656, ca. 1656
Oil on canvas, 49⅝ x 69⅝" (126 x 177 cm)
Museo Nazionale di San Martino, Naples

OPPOSITE TOP:
Carpaccio (ca. 1455–1523/26)
Venice, 1516
Oil on canvas, 51⅛ x 144⅞" (130 x 368 cm)
Palazzo Ducale, Venice

OPPOSITE BOTTOM:
Viviano Codazzi (1603/4–1670) and Filippo
Lauri (1623–1694)
Perspective with the Massacre of the Innocents, ca. 1656
Oil on canvas, 38 x 50⅛" (96.5 x 127.3 cm)
Bayerische Staatsgemäldesammlungen, Alte
Pinakothek, Munich

Canaletto (1697–1768)
Bacino di San Marco, ca. 1738
Oil on canvas, 49 x 80½"
(124.5 x 204.5 cm)
Museum of Fine Arts, Boston
Abbott Lawrence Fund,
Seth K. Sweetser Fund, and
Charles Edward French Fund

Canaletto (1697–1768)
*Bacino di San Marco with Bucintoro
on Ascension Day*, ca. 1729
Oil on canvas, 71⅝ x 102" (182 x 259 cm)
Crespi Collection, Milan

Bernardo Bellotto (1720–1780)
View of the Village of Gazzada, 1744
Oil on canvas, 25⅝ x 39⅜" (65 x 100 cm)
Pinacoteca di Brera, Milan

Giovanni Paolo Pannini (1691–1765)
The Roman Forum, 1749
Oil on canvas, 39¾ x 66⅛" (101 x 168 cm)
Gemäldegalerie, Staatliche Museen, Berlin

24.
Arresting Time

Still-life painting

Caravaggio's illustrious early patron, Vincenzo Giustiniani, records the artist's opinion that it was as difficult to make a good painting of flowers as one of figures. The picture to which he was evidently referring is lost, but it is described by his rival painter and biographer, Giovanni Baglione, as showing "a carafe of flowers filled with water in which was excellently depicted the reflection of a window and other objects in the room, and on those flowers are dew drops imitated with exquisite diligence. And this work [Caravaggio] said was the most beautiful he had ever made." Caravaggio had a notorious sense of irony, and he was a confirmed nonconformist. In point of fact, he painted few still lifes—only one, the *Still Life of a Basket of Fruit* in the Ambrosiana, Milan, survives—and the comment was certainly made for effect, for by the seventeenth century it was widely agreed that the highest kind of painting involved the depiction of an important subject or theme from ancient history or the Bible. Such a picture, it was felt, demanded all of an artist's abilities: his mastery of the human figure, the depiction of architecture and landscape, and such still-life embellishments as might be necessary. Viewed in this light, portraiture, landscape painting, genre, and still-life painting were distinctly inferior, and in most theoretical treatises they occupy descending positions in an established hierarchy. Caravaggio's comment was directed at this prejudice, and it proclaimed the primacy of skill and artistry over theory.

Caravaggio's *Still Life of a Basket of Fruit* may, in this respect, be seen as a theoretical broadside. The dried, curling leaves and blemished fruits constituted as strong an attack on the notion of ideal or perfected beauty, exalting truth to nature, as any of his unidealized nudes. This did not prejudice the person for whom it was painted, the reforming cardinal of Milan, Federigo Borromeo, who described it admiringly, noting that he would have loved to obtain a similar work but could find nothing to match its incomparable beauty.

Caravaggio's *Basket of Fruit* is usually seen as marking a turning point in the history of Italian still-life painting, which thenceforth took up the challenge of counterfeiting nature. It is, at the same time, the culmination of a process that began at least two centuries earlier. Unfortunately, the early stages of Italian still-life painting have all but disappeared and can only be reconstructed on the basis of documents, of details in larger works, and of those miraculous jigsaw puzzles of colored woods by which carpenters transformed sacristy cupboards and choir stalls into inlaid still lifes, landscapes, and architectural vistas.

One of the earliest notices of an independent still life dates from 1506, when Isabella d'Este was sent, among other things, "a painting full of fruit" by the Bolognese artist Antonio da Crevelcore who, the correspondent wittily remarked, took considerably longer than nature to produce his work. We can only guess at the appearance of the picture, since all of Crevelcore's paintings that survive are either religious subjects or portraits. What is perhaps the earliest surviving still life is a small panel showing a dead partridge and mail gauntlets painted two years earlier by the Venetian Jacopo de'Barbari. So unprecedented is this exercise in trompe l'oeil that it has been questioned whether the picture is not, after all, a fragment from a larger composition. The 1506 notice of Crevelcore's work suggests that we should not be surprised at the existence of independent still-life paintings at this date. After all, every educated patron was aware of the fact that one of the most famous works by the ancient artist Zeuxis showed a bunch of grapes whose realism was such that birds tried to peck them. Throughout its history Italian still-life painting placed a premium on deceiving the eye.

A second element comes into play in Italian still lifes—one shared with northern painting but possibly developed independently: the *vanitas* theme. It is probably not coincidental that the earliest surviving still life of fruit, a dish of peaches by the Milanese Ambrogio Figino, bears on its reverse an inscription alluding to the perishability of fruit—to fruit as a symbol of transient pleasures. The picture was painted about the same time as Caravaggio's lost still life of a carafe of flowers, which may have carried a similar meaning.

One cannot help but note the fact that each of these early examples was by a north Italian artist, for it was in northern Italy, and especially in Lombardy, that still-life painting first attracted major artists, although Rome and Naples, where Caravaggio was active, were not far behind. Among the earliest Lombard specialists in still life were the Milanese woman Fede Galizia, a contemporary of Caravaggio, and the Bergamasque Evaristo Baschenis. Baschenis was both a priest and a musician, and his beautifully arranged compositions of musical instruments, juxtaposing the upturned belly of a well-crafted lute with the rectangular surface of a spinet or the curves of a violin, the yellowed pages of a musical manuscript, the rich texture of an Anatolian carpet, and an occasional fruit or piece of sculpture, have an almost meta-physical quality that goes well beyond mere technical mastery. He loved finger marks wiped through a layer of dust, an obvious allusion to the passage of time (music, of course, is the symbol par excellence of transient pleasures and as such is frequently associated in poetry with love). It is probable that Baschenis knew some work by Caravaggio that had still-life elements—whether he went to Rome, where he could have seen one of the two versions Caravaggio painted of a lute player is not known—but the poetry of his pictures is his own creation.

Perhaps the most poignant *vanitas* still life of the seventeenth century is that painted by the Neapolitan Salvator Rosa, in which the arts, symbolized by a broken statue; music, alluded to by a rolled sheet of paper with notes; and learning, signified by an abandoned book, lie in disarray around a skull, painted with that morose sensitivity and reflectiveness that characterize much of Rosa's finest work (Alte Pinacotek, Munich; see chapter 13).

Together with portraiture, still-life painting was one of those genres in which women excelled, in part because it did not require their awkward and frequently banned presence in drawing academies, where models posed nude. In addition to Fede Galizia, with her delicate, muted touch, there was the central Italian Giovanna Garzoni, whose considerable fame was based on her abilities as a miniaturist. Her still lifes are, in fact, painted on parchment, and they combine the acuteness of the botanical illustrator with an uncommon gift for characterization. Her still life of an old man with two chickens standing behind a plateau on which are spread fruits, vegetables, and meats, is described in an early inventory as showing an old man from Artimio, a Medicean estate, and it is a fair assumption that the man is a portrait of a peas-ant. Typical of her egalitarian outlook is the attention she lavished on the wonderfully self-possessed dog. Garzoni's works were especially appreciated by the grand duke of Florence, Ferdinand II de'Medici, his brother Cardinal Giancarlo, and Prince Leopoldo de'Medici. For a subsequent generation of Medici grand dukes and princes, Bartolomeo Bimbi carried out his imaginative visual inventories of the rare and abun-dant fruits grown on their estates, reminding us of the link between still-life painting and an interest in the natural sciences, so popular in seventeenth-century courts.

Still-life painting flourished throughout Italy in the seventeenth and eighteenth centuries, but in Naples it achieved an imaginative extravagance that would be hard to match. Luca Forte's *Still Life with Fruit* in Sarasota overwhelms by its sheer superabundance and wit: a finch carrying a string to its mate spells out a dedication to Don Giuseppe Carafa, the brother of the duke of Maddaloni. For an almost olfactory visual effect, Porpora's crisply painted flowers have never been equaled. On the other hand, Giovanni Recco and his nephew Giuseppe sometimes add a calmer, quieter note to these opulent displays.

Yet, for a quality of domestic intimacy—a directness that announces the concerns of nineteenth-century painting—one must return to northern Italy: to Arcangelo Resani's extraordinary painting of a spotted dog curled up next to a reed basket and two game birds, and Giacomo Ceruti's elegantly simple *Still Life with Lobsters* (Pinacoteca di Brera, Milan). These works, painted in the eighteenth century, could not be farther removed from the prevalent rococo flourishes of contemporary history painting, and they are a poignant reminder that still-life painting in Italy could convey an outlook on everyday life as com-pelling as any other form of expression. They also demonstrate that still-life painting in Italy could vie with the sobriety of Chardin. But the true link is between Resani's spare compositions and those of Giorgio Morandi in the twentieth century (see chapter 27).

Jacopo de'Barbari (ca. 1440–before 1515)
Still Life with Dead Birds, 1504
Oil on wood, 20½ x 16¾" (52 x 42.5 cm)
Bayerische Staatsgemäldesammlungen, Alte
Pinakothek, Munich

Giovanna Garzoni (1600–1670)
Old Man of Artimius, ca. 1650–60
Tempera on parchment,
10⅝ x 13¾" (27 x 35 cm)
Galleria Palatina, Palazzo Pitti, Florence

Caravaggio (1571–1610)
Still Life of a Basket of Fruit, ca. 1600
Oil on canvas, 12¼ x 18½" (31 x 47 cm)
Pinacoteca Ambrosiana, Milan

Bartolomeo Bimbi (1648–1730)
Varieties of Cherries, 1699
Oil on canvas, 45⅝ x 61" (116 x 155 cm)
Galleria Palatina, Palazzo Pitti, Florence

OPPOSITE TOP:
Paolo Porpora (1617–1670/80)
Still Life with Fruits and Flowers, ca. 1640
Oil on canvas, 38⅝ x 50⅞" (98 x 129 cm)
Museo Nazionale di Capodimonte, Naples

OPPOSITE BOTTOM:
Luca Forte (ca. 1625–1655)
Still Life with Fruit, ca. 1640–47
Oil on canvas, 31 x 41¼" (78.7 x 104.7 cm)
The John and Mable Ringling Museum of
Art, Sarasota, Florida

OPPOSITE TOP:
Giovanni Battista Recco (ca. 1615–1660)
Still Life with Goat's Head, ca. 1640–50
Oil on canvas, 27⅛ x 39⅜" (69 x 100 cm)
Museo Nazionale di Capodimonte, Naples

OPPOSITE BOTTOM:
Evaristo Baschenis (1617–1677)
Still Life with Musical Instruments, ca. 1660–70
Oil on canvas, 34¼ x 45½" (87 x 115 cm)
Accademia Carrara, Bergamo

Arcangelo Resani (1670–1740)
Dog and a Basket, ca. 1700–1740
Oil on canvas, 22⅞ x 28¾" (58 x 73 cm)
Pinacoteca Comunale, Faenza

25.
The Third Estate and Private Pleasures

Genre painting

Tourists on holiday in Italy would do well to redirect their attention from the masterpieces of religious and mythological art that fill the museums and churches of Florence, Venice, and Rome to those remarkable works of "decorative art," the inlaid choir stalls and sacristy cupboards that are the glory of the carpenter's trade. If they do so, they will find themselves in a world scarcely imagined, in which the Madonna is only an occasional presence and the saints are frequently pushed aside by scenes dedicated to deserted landscape vistas, empty city squares, shelves stocked with chalices, cruets, books, musical instruments, and astrolabes, and figures in everyday dress who appear behind fictive windows playing the recorder, singing, or simply "hanging out." In the choir stalls of the monastery of Monte Oliveto Maggiore, southeast of Siena, the choir stalls and lectern contain panels showing a spotted cat sitting complacently on a fictive ledge before a river landscape, three finches hopping about behind a Renaissance arch, and Olivetan monks reading. These scenes were carried out in the early sixteenth century, at a time when painting was still largely concerned with devotional themes, mythological subjects, and portraiture, and they serve as a potent reminder that any view of Renaissance art based exclusively on those paintings that have survived is incomplete.

One of the very rare pictures to take up the themes encountered in choir stalls is Lorenzo Costa's *Concert*, probably painted in the 1480s. It shows three figures, two male and one female, who sing a madrigal from a part book laid out on the ledge in front of them. It is known that at the court of Mantua, Costa decorated a room showing Isabella d'Este and her court "who, singing variously, make sweet harmony." There can be little doubt that the *Concert* is an allegory of harmony in the guise of a group portrait; it is not, strictly speaking, a genre picture. The same is almost certainly true of a beautiful picture by Titian showing the three ages of man in the guise of a concert (Galleria Palatina, Palazzo Pitti, Florence). In it three men of different ages, one of whom is a monk, exchange meaningful glances while a middle-aged figure strikes a symbolic chord on a spinet. In visual terms the distance may not seem great between these two pictures and that painted by Orazio Gentileschi about 1610, in which a young woman listens intently as she tunes her lute, but although it is possible that Gentileschi's ravishing picture was intended as an allegory of music or harmony (in Italian, the word for tuning, *accordare*, means literally to bring together), it is just as likely that he intended simply to show someone involved in their favorite pastime. Gentileschi's picture would then mark a crucial shift from disguised allegory to pure genre. That the matter remains ambiguous is indicative of the elasticity of these categories of painting.

Genre painting is the stepchild of Italian art, something that seems to have happened almost before it was noted. An appreciation for genre motifs certainly existed from an early moment: the fifteenth-century humanist Bartolomeo Fazio has left a description of a work by Pisanello in the Doges' Palace in Venice illustrating an episode of the history of Frederick Barbarossa's struggle with Pope Alexander III in which the detail of a priest "distorting his face with his fingers, and some boys laughing at this" seems to have impressed viewers almost more than the main scene. It will also be recalled that in the fifteenth century the Borromeos had a room in their palace in Milan decorated with women playing cards and a game of ball (see chapter 7). A century later we hear of the Cremonese painter Sofonisba Anguissola sending to Michelangelo a drawing of "a little girl laughing at a child who has put his hand in a basket of lobsters and been bitten by one of them." The drawing was later sent to Duke Cosimo I de'Medici and, miraculously enough, it survives in Naples. Not until much later, in Caravaggio's painting of a *Boy Bitten by a Lizard* (National Gallery, London), do we have a painting treating a similar theme.

We are bound to ask ourselves what it was Michelangelo saw in Sofonisba's drawing and why, having admired it, he did nothing like it himself. The answer to the first question is that he admired the invention—that is, the fantasy Sofonisba had shown in choosing so unusual a theme (the fact that she was a woman artist added to the curiosity)—and the way it exploited an everyday subject in the depiction of an expression. The answer to the second question seems to be that to Michelangelo it was one thing to exhibit this talent in a drawing but quite another to confuse the depiction of a subject from everyday life with Art, which aimed to reveal the Truth behind Nature. The seventeenth-century apologist for classicism, Giovan Pietro Bellori, was adamant on this point. According to him, Caravaggio's principal error was to have despised the great statues of antiquity and the example of Raphael and to have taken for his model the most plebeian of social outcasts, a gypsy fortune-teller—a member of what we might call the third estate—as a suitable subject for a picture. So strong was this prejudice that Bellori seems consciously to have censored from his biography of Annibale Carracci those low-life subjects the Bolognese artist is known to have treated as a youth: works like the *Butcher Shop*, in which for the first time genre painting was accorded the scale normally reserved for biblical or mythological themes (whether the picture is really an allegory has never been resolved).

Faced with the existence of genrelike pictures that seemed, on the surface, to have no edifying theme, the late-sixteenth-century archbishop of Bologna, Gabriele Paleotti, allowed that they were acceptable so long as the actions and figures they depicted were rendered ridiculous. His views on the matter were greatly indebted to Aristotle, who in the *Poetics* had noted that just as tragedy achieves its edifying effects through the portrayal of men better than ourselves, so comedy relies on the ludicrous and imitates "men who are inferior but not altogether vicious." In other words, comedy was simply the reverse side of tragedy and could edify through its exaggeration of the foibles of common people. Paleotti termed this kind of painting *pitture ridicole*—comic pictures—and throughout the following century a bond was forged between the presentation of farce on the stage and genre painting. Annibale Carracci's senior, Bartolomeo Passerotti, painted a picture of two women marketing their chickens that is precisely the sort Paleotti had in mind (Gemäldegalerie, Berlin). It satirizes the ridiculous libido of an old croon selling her "goods" by showing a cock comically strutting behind her.

One does not have to do much scratching to find a moral intent, such as that in Passerotti's picture, below the surface of most genre paintings. Even Caravaggio's *Fortune-Teller* teaches the obvious lesson that those who trust such a shady character as a gypsy might as well kiss their valuables goodbye: the enamored youth is, in fact, losing his ring to the exotic enchantress. The real key to the picture, however, lies not in the theme but in Caravaggio's realism, which his contemporary Gaspare Murtola understood perfectly: "You have painted [this gypsy] so that she seems alive; so that living and breathing, others believe her."

There are many pictures in which a more caustic tone than that of Caravaggio's painting is adopted, but the reprimand is usually transparent. This is so even in Piazzetta's *Fortune-Teller*, in which the conceited silliness of the female victim is completely winning. It is a short step from pictures like these that pretend to teach commonplace lessons (what we would call "street smartness") to paintings that transform genre into a means of social commentary. Giuseppe Maria Crespi's *Flea Hunt*, known in a number of versions, was long appreciated for its apparent depiction of a slice of ordinary life. It is, however, just possible that the picture once formed part of a larger series tracing the rise and fall of a singer (a spinet is shown at the left). Of this series the eighteenth-century critic Zanotti made the following predictable remark: "I know that the pictures of this series I saw made me split my sides with laughing." What sets Crespi's picture apart from earlier "comic pictures," as well as from the far more scathing class humor of Gaspare Traversi's contemporary *Drawing Lesson*, is the sympathetic attention Crespi has lavished on the accouterments of this simple dwelling: the intertwined garlic hanging on the wall, the crockery, and the oil lamp with a rosary above the fashionable spaniel (the source of the woman's fleas?). In a work such as Giacomo Ceruti's *Beggars*, this sort of acute observation seems almost to amount to a social manifesto arising from the artist's sympathy for the dispossessed. No other eighteenth-century picture brings us so close

to the deprivation that was the common lot of a large segment of the population and to the resultant hardened character of peasants and beggars.

Like the Bolognese Crespi, the Lombard Ceruti, and the Neapolitan Traversi, the Venetian Pietro Longhi also played upon distinctions of class in exploring the humorous side of the human condition. However, in his hands the almost cruel mockery that was Traversi's specialty and the eye to truthfulness that is the keynote of Ceruti's work is exchanged for a lighthearted, polite humor that never oversteps the boundaries of good taste. His peasants would never trouble the almost nonexistent social conscience of his patrons, and the failings he exposes in the upper classes are always forgivable. In the *Apothecary,* a woman seeks a cure for a toothache while, in the background, a priest and a gentleman wait their turn. The picture has the appearance of straightforward reportage, and, indeed, Longhi's work has been compared to the plays of his great contemporary Goldoni. However, he lacked Goldoni's biting wit and sense of individual character that transforms genre into social commentary. Domenico Tiepolo's enchanting *Dance in the Country* and Filippo Falciatore's *Dancing the Tarantella at Mergellina* are in some ways more revealing portrayals of eighteenth-century life precisely because they disavow any intention beyond that of giving pleasure.

There could be no greater warning of the danger of underestimating the power of allegorical genre painting than Bartolomeo Schedoni's depiction of *Charity* in the guise of a turbaned woman distributing bread to beggars and Ribera's depiction of the *Sense of Smell* as a peasant holding up a sliced onion, his eyes tearing at the fumes. In both, the allegorical content served as a lens through which two very different artists commented on the life around them. If we find in Schedoni's picture a moving depiction of a blind man, in Ribera's we cannot help but be shocked at the almost ruthless characterization of a rustic and, of necessity, uncouth member of the third estate. The same is true of the series of thirteen pictures painted by Domenico Fetti for the Gonzaga family in Mantua, in which parables from the Bible are interpreted in terms of everyday life. In Fetti's illustration of the parable of the mote and the beam, the result is almost comical, as a man seated in an elevated position disregards a threatening beam to point out a mote in his companion's eye. These are pictures conditioned by prejudiced views, but they are no less forceful and revealing for all that.

Orazio Gentileschi (1563–1639)
The Lute Player, ca. 1610
Oil on canvas, 56 ½ x 50⅝" (143.5 x 128.8 cm)
National Gallery of Art, Washington
Ailsa Mellon Bruce Fund

OPPOSITE:
Bartolomeo Schedoni (1578–1615)
Charity (The Alm), ca. 1611–12
Oil on canvas, 71⅝ x 49 ¼" (182 x 125 cm)
Gallerie Nazionali di Capodimonte, Naples

Jusepe de Ribera (1591–1652)
Sense of Smell, ca. 1613–15
Oil on canvas, 45¾ x 34⅝" (115 x 88 cm)
Private Collection, Madrid

OPPOSITE TOP:
Annibale Carracci (1560–1609)
The Butcher Shop, ca. 1583
Oil on canvas, 74⅞ x 67⅜" (190 x 171 cm)
The Governing Body, Christ Church, Oxford

OPPOSITE BOTTOM:
Bernardo Strozzi (1581–1644)
The Cook, ca. 1630
Oil on canvas, 69⅝ x 94⅞" (177 x 241 cm)
Palazzo Rosso, Genoa

OPPOSTIE TOP:
Gaspare Traversi (ca. 1722–1770)
The Drawing Lesson, ca. 1760
Oil on canvas, 59¾ x 80⁵⁄₁₆" (151.7 x 204 cm)
The Nelson-Atkins Museum of Art,
Kansas City, Missouri
Gift of the Samuel H. Kress Foundation

OPPOSITE BOTTOM:
Giacomo Ceruti (1698–1767)
The Two Beggars, ca. 1730–40
Oil on canvas, 53 x 68⅛"
(134.5 x 173 cm)
Pinacoteca Civica
Tosio-Martinengo, Brescia

Piazzetta (1683–1754)
The Fortune-Teller, 1740
Oil on canvas, 60⅝ x 44⅞" (154 x 114 cm)
Accademia, Venice

Domenico Fetti (1588/89–1623)
Parable of the Mote and the Beam, ca. 1618–21
Oil on wood, 24⅛ x 17⅜" (61.3 x 44.1 cm)
The Metropolitan Museum of Art, New York
Rogers Fund, 1991

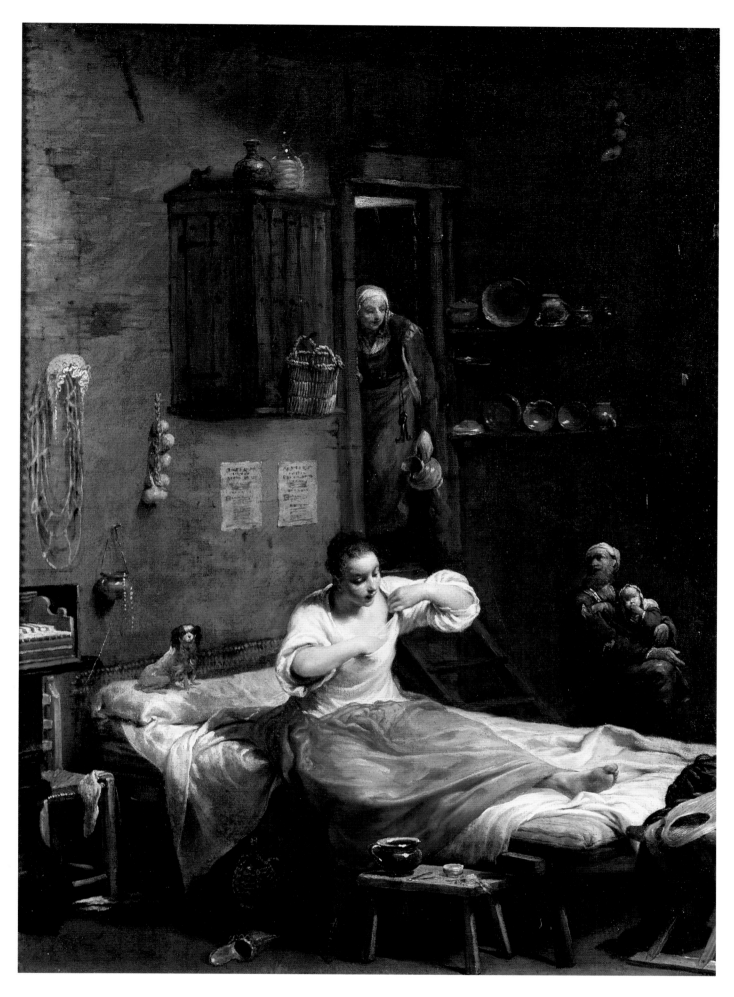

Giuseppe Maria Crespi (1665–1747)
The Flea Hunt, ca. 1728
Oil on canvas, 21⅝ x 16⅛" (55 x 41 cm)
Musée du Louvre, Paris

281

26.
Toward a New Naturalism

The Macchiaioli and their contemporaries

Despite the regional divisions of Italy and their domination by one or another of the major European powers, principally Spain, Italian society at the end of the eighteenth century was remarkably uniform. Whether the Republic of Venice, the duchies of Milan and Tuscany, Papal Rome, or the kingdom of Naples, wealth and power were in the hands of a few, while the vast majority of the population lived in abject poverty. Corruption was rife, both in secular and in ecclesiastical spheres; crime, rampant; and the prospect for change, dim. This state of affairs was dramatically altered by Napoleon's invasion in 1796—three hundred years after the troops of Charles VIII had signaled the end of Italian independence. Venice may have lost its freedom to Austria, but elsewhere old political systems were swept aside in a tide of republicanism. The pope abandoned Rome and the king of Naples sailed to Sicily. The immediate effects of this breath of fresh air were short-lived (they were, in fact, premature, since Napoleon had no intention of liberating Italy); after the final defeat of Napoleon at Waterloo in 1815, the European powers tried to reassert the status quo, which meant a divided and subjugated Italy. However, the long-term effect was irreversible. A sense of nationhood and a resolve to free Italy from foreign domination, the like of which had not been felt since the early sixteenth century, was kindled. This movement, known as the Risorgimento (that is, revival or awakening) dominated all aspects of intellectual life and revealed itself, initially, in a new awareness of the past. Alessandro Manzoni's great novel *The Betrothed (I promessi sposi)*, and Verdi's opera *Nabucco*, performed at La Scala in 1842 to wild acclaim, defined the Italian consciousness in the same way Dante's *Divine Comedy* and Michelangelo's frescoes on the vault of the Sistine Chapel had in the fourteenth and sixteenth centuries. Nothing comparable to these works was produced in the visual arts, in part because the historicizing idiom through which this national awareness was expressed was already a timeworn convention.

There were, of course, a number of distinguished painters, such as Francesco Hayez in Milan and the landscape painters in Naples known as the school of Posillipo, but only in Florence, in the years immediately preceding the unification of Italy, did a truly significant movement arise. As was to be so often the case in the nineteenth century, the intellectual center of this group was a bar, the Caffè Michelangiolo on Via Larga (the present-day Via Cavour), where Florentine nationalists, intellectuals, and artists met. Some of these artists had fought with Garibaldi in 1848 and fought with him again in the great 1860 campaign that led to the unification of Italy, completed in 1870 with the entrance in Rome of Vittorio Emanuele II (between 1865 and 1871 Florence was the capital of the new kingdom of Italy). The Neapolitan Giuseppe Abbati lost his eye in the Battle of Capua, and the Florentine Raffaello Sernesi died of wounds inflicted by the Austrians in 1866. What bound these artists together was their intense patriotism and their desire to create a means of expression that reflected their belief in a free, modern, and republican Italy. A number of them tried their hand at historical subjects, some with considerable success. Eduardo Borrani, an apprentice of the restorer who uncovered Giotto's frescoes in Santa Croce, was awarded a gold medal for his painting of the fifteenth-century conspiracy of the Pazzi against the Medici (a subject with strong republican overtones), while Silvestro Lega exhibited a picture treating a subject from Chateaubriand's *The Martyrs*. Giovanni Fattori was an avid reader of the popular historical romances by Sir Walter Scott and Victor Hugo and treated such literary subjects as Mary Stuart on the battlefield at Crookstone (Sir Walter Scott had, of course, been a primary source for Donizetti's operas). These culminated in his prize-winning painting celebrating the Battle of Magenta, a crucial event in the Italian war of independence. However, by the late 1850s the attention of these men turned from historical painting, with its associations of the art of the academies, to painting outdoors from nature. Inspiration was drawn from contemporary French, seventeenth-century Dutch, and eighteenth-century English painting, which could be seen in the Demidoff collection in Florence, and it was further encouraged by reports from Paris of the work of the Barbizon School (Daubigny and, later, Corot were particularly admired). It would, however, be wrong to see in this interest in landscape painting a pale reflection of French practice, and it is important to distinguish their work from the virtually contemporary experiments of the Impressionists.

Today, when amateurs set up their easels in parks and fields as a matter of course, it is difficult to appreciate that painting landscape directly from nature could be considered revolutionary, but if the conventions that ruled painting through the eighteenth century are borne in mind, it is not difficult to see the defiance and egalitarian attitude this art represented. One of the group's most eloquent early supporters, Massimo d'Azeglio, declared, "The landscape painters all chant together 'Rome or death,' but when they take up their brushes, the only thing they don't paint is Italy. The magnificent Italian landscape, the glorious light, the rich hues of the sky over our heads and the earth we tread; no one considers these things worthy of being painted." It was this challenge the Florentine group set themselves.

To insure the truthfulness of tone and convey the quality of immediacy that stood at the heart of their venture, a small-scale format and sketchlike brushwork were adopted—what in the seventeenth century was called a *macchia* (a term that also refers to the individual daubs of color). In a fashion typical of avant-garde movements, the name of the group, the Macchiaioli, derived from the criticism of a hostile reviewer in 1862. Fortunately, we have it from one of their own, Adriano Cecioni, what these artists had in mind. "What is the *macchia,* in the final analysis? A harmony of tone . . . aimed at capturing a specific feeling in the mind of the painter, and at making the imagination the focus of his artistic productivity. The *macchia* is the *sine qua non* of the painting, its indispensable and essential ingredient, which can sometimes make one forget the painting's other flaws. . . . To execute and finish a painting means nothing more than a gradual narrowing of the distance between the artist and the object itself. . . . [Yet] if that first fundamental harmonic ingredient is missing . . . then the finished work—no matter how large it may be— will never be able to move the spectator or to stir any emotion at all in him. A single naked *macchia,* on the other hand, is fully capable of stirring up such emotions."

It is generally true that the finest Macchiaioli works are those painted on panels less than a foot wide: works like Raffaello Sernesi's *Rooftops in the Sun,* painted about 1861, with its purity of color and clarity of composition—almost a premonition of what Giorgio Morandi was to do in the twentieth century. Or the equally compelling view of a cloister during its restoration by Giuseppe Abbati (the restoration of the great historical landmarks was a typical product of the new awareness of Italy's past). Although attempts have been made to read political or social meanings into these works, Abbati seems to have been more fascinated with the marble slabs and the resting worker than with nationalistic associations with the city's medieval past.

In 1861 Diego Martelli, a regular at the Caffè Michelangiolo, inherited a vast estate along the coast south of Livorno, and it was to Castiglioncello, to the Piagentina countryside on the southern outskirts of Florence, and to the fertile flatlands of the Maremma in southern Tuscany that the Macchiaioli went for inspiration. Silvestro Lega's *The Pergola,* showing a group of women taking coffee in their garden after lunch, and Eduardo Borrani's depiction of the Mugnone, a tributary of the Arno river, were done in the Piagentina, at a time when the revolutionary passions and optimism that reigned in the years 1848–60 had given way to a sense of melancholy and disappointment at the political compromises and stagnation that followed the unification. They epitomize perfectly Cecioni's remarks about capturing the "feeling in the mind of the painter."

Giovanni Fattori, the most gifted of the Macchiaioli, began his outdoor works painting French soldiers camped in the Cascine outside Florence, but between 1861 and 1867 he returned to his native Livorno, from which he made trips to the pastureland of the Maremma. There the great white oxen that are still a familiar sight particularly captured his imagination—a potent and, it then seemed, a more enduring symbol of Italian life than even the great medieval monuments of Florence. To fully appreciate these works, it is now necessary to suppress our own romantic associations with peasant life that are a product of the industrialization of Italy, which then lay in the distant future. Fattori sought to record life by capturing a moment of experience, such as women (all of them faceless) taking refuge from the strong sun beneath a rotunda at Palmieri. His portrait of his stepdaughter, done long after the Macchiaioli had disbanded and the Caffè Michelangiolo had closed its doors, shows how faithful he remained in his commitment to perceptual truth. He lived until 1908, by which time the impulse behind the Macchiaioli had been replaced by Divisionism, with its emphasis on painting as an optical science through the use of complementary colors. Fattori had little sympathy for this style, which he thought exhibited no humanitarian face. It had been some time since the gifted but over-facile Giovanni Boldini had cashed in on his talent in Paris, painting society portraits. In the 1860s he had been associated with the Macchiaioli and produced works of a very different order. The Neapolitan Giuseppe de Nittis also abandoned Italy for Paris, where a highbrow Impressionism replaced a native Italian style.

For those who remained in Italy, the political and economic promises of the Risorgimento faded into the past, replaced with economic decline and peasant and workers' movements. Over one hundred rioters were killed in Milan in 1898 by the repression of General Bava Beccaris. It was against this backdrop that Pellizza da Volpedo, who had spent some time with Fattori, rose to become the spokesman of a new generation. His *The Fourth Estate* stands as a signpost to the disillusionment of the Italian intelligentsia. The vehicle was Divisionism, which, however, for him was an instrument of "social illumination." Pellizza believed that "the truth that appears before us always comes into conflict with the truth contained in the harmony of our mind," and it was the latter truth—the ideal truth—he espoused. This subversion of the more objective reality of the Macchiaioli to the demands of the artist's subjective self allied Pellizza and other Divisionists, such as Giovanni Segatini, to twentieth-century art.

Raffaello Sernesi (1838–1866)
Rooftops in the Sun, 1861
Oil on cardboard, 4⅞ x 7½" (12.3 x 19 cm)
Galleria Nazionale d'Arte Antica, Rome

OPPOSITE TOP:
Giuseppe Abbati (1836–1868)
Cloister, 1863
Oil on cardboard, 7⅝ x 10" (19.3 x 25.2 cm)
Galleria d'Arte Moderna, Palazzo Pitti, Florence

OPPOSITE BOTTOM:
Eduardo Borrani (1833–1905)
The Mugnone, ca. 1865
Oil on wood, 10 x 15 ⅛" (25.5 x 38.5 cm)
Galleria Nazionale d'Arte Moderna, Rome

286

Silvestro Lega (1826–1895)
The Pergola, 1868
Oil on canvas, 29½ x 36¾" (75 x 93.5 cm)
Pinacoteca di Brera, Milan

OPPOSITE:
Giovanni Fattori (1825–1908)
Portrait of His Stepdaughter, 1889
Oil on canvas, 28 x 21⅝" (71 x 55 cm)
Galleria d'Arte Moderna, Palazzo Pitti, Florence

Giuseppe Pellizza da Volpedo (1868–1907)
The Fourth Estate, 1901
Oil on canvas, 216½ x 111⅜" (550 x 283 cm)
Galleria d'Arte Moderna, Milan

OPPOSITE TOP:
Giovanni Fattori (1825–1908)
The Oxcart, 1870
Oil on canvas, 15¾ x 41" (40 x 104 cm)
Galleria d'Arte Moderna, Palazzo Pitti, Florence

OPPOSITE BOTTOM:
Giuseppe de Nittis (1846–1884)
Lunch at Posillipo, 1908
Oil on canvas, 43¾ x 67¾" (111 x 172 cm)
Civiche Raccolte d'Arte, Milan

27.
A Manifesto for the Future

Painting between 1900 and 1919

However modern the technique of the Macchiaioli now seems when compared to the academic traditions against which they had rebelled, their love of landscape and of the slow pace of the country and their faith in the experience of an objective reality bound them to a preindustrial, premodern point of view. In point of fact, at the turn of the century Italy was still an agricultural nation in which industry was in its infancy, concentrated in the area encompassed by Milan, Turin, and Genoa. Not surprisingly, it was in Turin that that harbinger of modern painting, Pellizza da Volpedo (see chapter 26), associated with a group of intellectuals. Guglielmo Ferrero was the author of a book on the psychological laws of Symbolism, while Giovanni Cena was a Socialist writer and poet. Twentieth-century Italian art was born from social activism, a new understanding of the psychology of perception, and a commitment to making art a mouthpiece for change. Works like Pellizza da Volpedo's *The Fourth Estate* employ a nineteenth-century technique derived from Impressionist and Postimpressionist painting (Divisionism) as a vehicle for political reform. Giacomo Balla's *Bankruptcy (Fallimento)* is an expression of despair in the face of political and social disintegration.

The same year *The Fourth Estate* was exhibited in Rome, in 1907, Pellizza committed suicide. Just two years later, on February 20, 1909, Filippo Marinetti published his *Manifesto for Futurism* in the French daily *Le Figaro.* In it there is no hint of the malaise that marks the work of Pellizza and Balla. Marinetti had a faculty for striking the hyperbolic posture necessary to set things on a new track (in this he resembled Mussolini, who he shamefully supported to the end), and in the *Manifesto del Futurismo* he audaciously turned his back on despair and on Italy's past, wholeheartedly embracing a confident, modernist vision of the future. "It is from Italy," he declared, "that we now establish Futurism with this manifesto of overwhelming and burning violence, because we want to free this country from its fetid gangrene of professors, archaeologists, antiquarians, and rhetoricians." "Aggressive motion, feverish insomnia, the swift pace, the fatal leap, the slap, and the punch" were the remedies he prescribed.

In Milan the following year he met the painters Umberto Boccioni, Luigi Russolo, and Carlo Carrà, young artists seeking a way out of the impasse of Balla's Divisionist work (after working with Balla in Rome, Boccioni had fled what he saw as the provincial life of Italy to Paris and then went on to Russia at the invitation of friends he met in the French capital). Under Boccioni's leadership, these artists issued a *Manifesto of Futurist Painters* on February 11, 1910, signed also by Giacomo Balla and Boccioni's close friend Gino Severini, then resident in Paris. Addressed "To the young artists of Italy!" the manifesto declared all out warfare against the past: "We want to fight to the bitter end against the fanatical, thoughtless, and purely snobbish religious faith in the past stoked by the nefarious existence of the museums. We are rebelling against the sluggishly supine admiration for old canvases, old statues, old objects, and against the enthusiasm for everything worm-eaten, rotting with filth, eaten away by time. . . . We are nauseated by the despicable sloth that, ever since the sixteenth century, has let our artists survive only through the incessant reworking of the glories of the past. . . . Italy is being reborn, and in the wake of the political resurgence an intellectual resurgence is taking place."

The still-hazy goals of the Futurists amounted at this point to an agenda "to destroy the cult of the past" and "to exalt every form of originality, even if foolhardy, even if extremely violent," and, finally, "to render and magnify the life of today, incessantly and tumultuously transformed by science triumphant." With this document, confidence replaced despair and direction was given to art, thought, and fashion in Italy for the entire twentieth century. In no other country has the love-hate relationship with its cultural heritage been as intense.

At the time, none of the signatories had a clear notion how to achieve their goal. In Italy, art and theory have always developed hand in hand, and Futurism was no exception. Futurist paintings were the expression of a theoretical point of view rather than the result of the working out of purely formal problems. The distinction was not lost on Gino Severini, who wrote his "comrades" from Paris that "those who, strictly speaking, are Cubists do not even know why they are called thus. . . . Their endeavor is certainly heroic, but infantile. I allude to the goal that they have set themselves: to paint an object from several sides or dissected. The engineers have resolved that question in a more complete fashion, and there is no need to go back to it." Despite this assertion of independence from Paris and the artistic events there, Italian artists nonetheless felt the pull of French modernism, and what they achieved is best seen as a dialogue—sometimes hostile, sometimes open—with art in the Parisian capital.

By April Boccioni had found his way. "Everything is in movement," he wrote in the *Technical Manifesto*, "everything rushes forward, everything is in constant swift change. . . . Because images persist on the retina, things in movement multiply, change form, follow one upon the other like vibrations within the space they traverse. . . . Our new awareness no longer lets us view man as the center of universal life. For us, a man's pain is interesting no less but no more than that of an electric light bulb . . . ; and the musicality of the line and folds of a modern garment have, for us, an emotional and symbolic power entirely like that the nude had for old masters."

With *Riot in the Galleria*, painted shortly after writing these words, Boccioni made a decisive step toward a new, modern style in which, however, his debt to French Postimpressionism and Italian Divisionism is still evident in his technique and use of complementary colors. In his encapsulation of café life, *The Laugh*, painted the following year, the transformation was complete. It is painting not of modern life but, in the words of a recent critic, "of sensations derived from observation of modern life." Although superficially reminiscent of Cubism, Boccioni's work explores a world of relationships in constant flux. The picture was defaced but not seriously damaged when it was exhibited in Milan in 1911, and the response to this "attack" is typical: "Undaunted we are continuing [the] battle." Boccioni later extended his subjects to movement itself. Giacomo Balla and Carlo Carrà were not far behind in opening their art to the dynamism of movement: the antithesis of the classical calm of Piero della Francesca, Raphael, and the Macchiaioli. Boccioni went to Paris in 1911, where he was dazzled both by the art he saw and the character of Parisian life. But when his work was exhibited there, it was received coldly since, inevitably, it was viewed in terms of Cubism (it should also be confessed that French intellectualism was not open to the rhetorical component of Futurist art and theory).

The heroic moment of Futurism was short-lived. With the outbreak of World War I in 1914, these activated artists found a new cause to channel their energies: this is not the first time and will certainly not be the last that militarism has seduced artists seeking a cause. Together with Marinetti, Boccioni joined the Cyclists' Battalion. He then signed on with the regular army, dying in 1916 from a fall off a horse. Boccioni's death was not the end of Futurism, but never again did the movement recapture its buoyantly outrageous optimism, and many of its members fell away.

Futurism was the expression of youthful passion and conviction: the standard bearer of Italian modernism. As such it has exerted a continuing attraction on young artists. But in the same years Boccioni and the circle around the demagogic figure of Marinetti were throwing over the baggage of the past, Giorgio de Chirico was finding in its visible remnants a means of exploring the world of associations—what he called the "primordial feeling of prehistory." He did this by using individually potent images from Italy's past—arcaded streets, large rectangular squares, Roman statues, and architectural fragments—placed in purposely enigmatic juxtapositions. That archenemy of modernism, perspective, with the tidy grid it imposed on life, was deployed in an irrational fashion to heighten the peculiarity of the conjunctions. De Chirico's pictures intentionally disconcert and delude (as well as elude) the viewer who tries to submit them to rational analysis, for their components are poetic similes or signs that draw upon a distant, collective memory. Whereas the Futurists proclaimed a painting of action, de Chirico investigated the world of the metaphysical: his are pictures of the mind filtered through the symbols of civilization and its myths.

De Chirico was trained not in Italy (he was born in Greece of Italian parents), but in Germany, where he and his writer-painter brother Alberto Savinio studied Nietzsche and Schopenhauer, attended performances of Wagner's operas, and admired the haunting, dreamlike paintings of the German romantic Arnold Böcklin. He brought to Italian painting a German tendency to intellectualize and a Nietzschean view of the artist as orphic seer and painting as oracle. His self-portrait completed in Florence in 1911 bears the Latin inscription *et quid amabo, nisi quod aenigma est?* (And what shall I love if not the enigma?). When he stayed in Turin in 1911—the city in which he knew Nietzsche had shown signs of metal ill-ness—he was fascinated less by the fast-growing industry than by the images the city presented: its expansive vistas and squares with monuments to the heroes of the Risorgimento, and the curious effect of its railway stations. His keen interest in Italian art of the past is evident in his *Self-Portrait* of 1913, which makes conscious reference to fifteenth-century profile portraits (see chapter 17).

The Metaphysical art of de Chirico and his brother exerted a strong and long-lasting influence—in some respects stronger even than Futurism. The poetic and psychological character of the images, with their evocation of the past, opened a number of avenues for development. In the early years of World War I Carlo Carrà turned from Futurism to a consciously naive style based on his study of early Renaissance artists. Then, in 1917, he was stationed in Ferrara, where he met de Chirico. Shortly thereafter he began producing Metaphysical pictures of extraordinary beauty, such as the hermetic *Enchanted Room,* with its composite dress form, milliner's head, fishing tackle, and mounted fish—all familiar elements of de Chirico's imagery. Boccioni had declared war on the genres of landscape and still-life painting, but in their work the Metaphysical painters affirmed the expressive potency of these art forms. It was to de Chirico and Carrà that the Bolognese Giorgio Morandi, the greatest Italian still-life painter of the twentieth century, owed the sense of mystery that pervades his work. He studied Carrà's paintings in photographs and was acquainted with de Chirico, but there is also in his work evidence of a careful study of such early Italian masters as Paolo Uccello, whose depictions of an objectified space Morandi greatly admired.

Art in Italy before World War I is defined by Futurism and Metaphysical painting, but the Italian who today enjoys the greatest popularity belonged to neither movement. It may, indeed, be questioned whether Amedeo Modigliani properly belongs in a history of Italian painting, for although he was trained in Italy, where he studied with the grand old master of the Macchiaioli, Giovanni Fattori, he moved to Paris in 1906, and his art is intimately bound with that of the French capital. His admiration for African masks and "primitive" sculpture was shared by Picasso and Brancusi, and his palette and brushwork were inspired by the work of Cézanne. His female nudes might be seen as an eloquent refutation of Boccioni's condemnation of this old-master theme (he had, in fact, declined signing the Futurist manifesto), but their context is Picasso's Paris, not Marinetti's Milan. And although there are in Modigliani's pictures occasional, distant echoes of the works of such early Italian masters as Duccio, Simone Martini, and the sculptor Tino da Camaino, which he studied in Florence, these can hardly be considered basic to his work. Only after his premature death in 1920 did his work gradually become known in Italy, and even then its influence on twentieth-century Italian painting has not been great.

Giacomo Balla (1871–1958)
Bankruptcy, 1902
Oil on canvas, 45⅝ x 63" (116 x 160 cm)
Museum Ludwig, Cologne

Umberto Boccioni (1882–1916)
Riot in the Galleria, 1910
Oil on canvas, 30¾ x 25 ⅛" (76.9 x 64 cm)
Pinacoteca di Brera, Milan
Gift of Emilio and Maria Jesi

Gino Severini (1883–1966)
Plastic Synthesis of the Idea "War," 1915
Oil on canvas, 23⅝ x 19⅝" (60 x 50 cm)
Bayerische Staatsgemäldesammlungen,
Staatsgalerie Moderner Kunst, Munich

OPPOSITE TOP:
Carlo Carrà (1881–1966)
The Station in Milan, 1909
Oil on canvas, 31 ½ x 35⅜" (80 x 90 cm)
Private Collection, Trent

OPPOSITE BOTTOM:
Umberto Boccioni (1882–1916)
The Laugh, 1911
Oil on canvas, 43⅜ x 57¼" (110.17 x 145.42 cm)
The Museum of Modern Art, New York
Gift of Herbert and Nannette Rothschild

OPPOSITE:
Carlo Carrà (1881–1966)
The Enchanted Room, 1917
Oil on canvas, 26¾ x 20½"
(68 x 52 cm)
Pinacoteca di Brera, Milan
Gift of Emilio and Maria Jesi

Giacomo Balla (1871–1958)
*Abstract Speed—The Car
Has Passed*, 1913
Oil on canvas, 102⅜ x 130¾"
(260 x 332 cm)
The Tate Gallery, London

Giorgio de Chirico (1888–1978)
The Soothsayer's Recompense, 1913
Oil on canvas, 53⅜ x 71" (136 x 181 cm)
Philadelphia Museum of Art
The Louise and Walter Arensberg
Collection

OPPOSITE:
Amedeo Modigliani (1884–1920)
Female Nude, 1916
Oil on canvas, 36⅜ x 23½" (92.4 x 59.8 cm)
Courtauld Institute Galleries, London

Giorgio Morandi (1890–1964)
Still Life, 1919
Oil on canvas, 23⅝ x 23¼" (60 x 59 cm)
Pinacoteca di Brera, Milan
Gift of Emilio and Maria Jesi

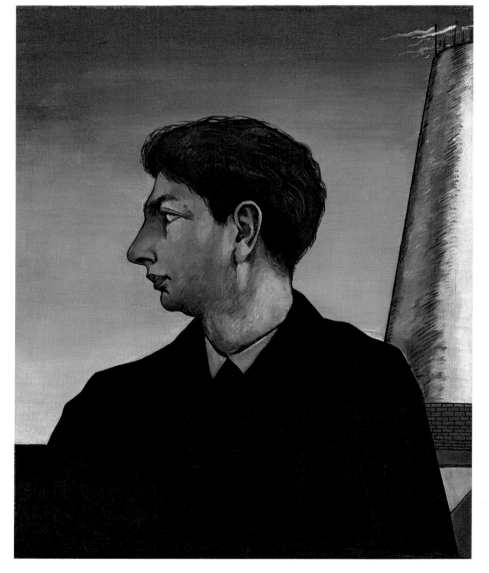

Giorgio de Chirico (1888–1978)
Self-Portrait, 1913
Oil on canvas, 34⅜ x 27½" (87.31 x 69.85 cm)
The Metropolitan Museum of Art, New York
Gift of Fania Marinoff, in memory of
Carl Van Vechten and Fania Marinoff, 1970

28.
Art under Fascism

Painting from 1922 to 1943

From the period of the Risorgimento on, art in Italy has never strayed far from those twin concerns of nationalism and politics. The Macchiaioli movement was born of the quest for Italian unity and a search for national identity; some of its protagonists had fought with Garibaldi. At the end of the nineteenth century, artists like Pellizza da Volpedo were advocates of social reform. In the early twentieth century, Futurism sought to transform Italy into a modern, industrial power. Nevertheless, none of these movements was associated with a particular political regime. With Mussolini's murder of the Socialist deputy Giacomo Matteotti and his creation of a dictatorship in 1925, three years after the march on Rome which brought him to power, the question of a state-sponsored style became inevitable. The issue was raised in 1926 in the journal *Critica fascista* by Giuseppe Bottai, later Mussolini's Minister of National Education. Typically, the Futurist propagandist Marinetti insisted that Futurism—no longer the vital movement it had been—was the proper vehicle (to his great discredit, Marinetti continued to support Mussolini even after the latter's forced resignation in Rome and the establishment of a puppet Fascist state at Salò, in northern Italy). The former Futurist Gino Severini also participated in the debate together with Margherita Sarfatti, until 1934 Mussolini's mistress and, unlike him, a person of culture and intellect. Sarfatti had sponsored a movement known as the Novecento (the 1900s) that sought to fuse classical traditions with modernism. In addition to Severini, the movement attracted the Futurist-turned-Metaphysical painter Carlo Carrà and, above all, Mario Sironi, who was to remain a staunch supporter of Mussolini to the end. The caliber of these artists stands in stark contrast to the heartless propagandistic painting Goebbels enforced in Nazi Germany and, indeed, the artistic culture of Fascist Italy remained surprisingly varied. There were unsuccessful and poorly organized attempts to impose some sort of uniformity, but it is indicative of the lack of central control that in 1940 and 1941 the state-sponsored Premio di Bergamo was awarded to the anti-Fascist Renato Guttuso. (A Communist, Guttuso was forced to flee Rome in 1943, returning the following year as a member of the Resistance.) It is thus possible to speak of art under Fascism without reference to a Fascist art.

To understand how men like Marinetti and Sironi could have associated themselves with a figure and movement that now appear both discredited and abhorrent, several factors must be borne in mind. The first is that in its early years Fascism presented a face of social reform and national unity. The second is that the call by Mussolini and his first Minister of Education, Giovanni Gentile, to intellectuals to abandon their ivory tower could not help but appeal to ideologues like Marinetti and to artists like Sironi. It is, perhaps, enough to note that in 1916 Sironi, together with Boccioni and Marinetti, had signed the manifesto of *Italian Pride (Orgoglio Italiano)* advocating "slaps, kicks, and gunshots in the back of the Italian artist or intellectual who hides beneath his talent like an ostrich behind its luxuriant plumes, and who fails to align his own pride with the military pride of his race." That statement was made at the outbreak of World War I, but it was followed by a proclamation of support for Mussolini—"the Man who will know how to value correctly the force of our Art dominating the world"—after the march on Rome, and it points up the shallowness in the political thinking of Marinetti and Sironi; a shallowness paralleled in the superficial modernism of Sironi's paintings, whose conservative vocabulary was based on an all-too-obvious study of Renaissance art. Sironi's paintings have the uncomfortable character of a marriage of convenience between tradition and modernism, and there is no mystery why he should have become a leading figure in the Novecento movement and a caricaturist for Mussolini's official press, *Il Popolo d'Italia*.

Yet, it would be wrong to interpret a resurgence of figurative painting and the renewed interest in the artistic heritage of the past as an indication of Fascist sympathies. These were, after all, the very years Picasso turned from the near abstraction of Synthetic Cubism to classically inspired compositions of monumental female figures. De Chirico's declaration in 1919 that he was a classical painter was accompanied by a study of Titian and classical art. In Paris, where he returned in 1924, de Chirico was much impressed by Picasso's neoclassicism. His pictures of these years are more loosely painted (sometimes to the point of formal degeneracy) and are more conventional: in Paris André Breton became the first of many who have championed the early work of de Chirico to the exclusion of his later painting. Carlo Carrà's poetic paintings of the late teens and twenties, with their conscious reference to the fourteenth-century frescoes of Giotto, reveal some of the same tendencies.

The artist who in many respects seems the most reactionary, Felice Casorati, had been arrested in 1923 for his association with the anti-Fascist Gobetti: the stark realism ("Magic Realism") of his work was based on a study of quattrocento painting, especially that of Piero della Francesca, then coming to wide notice through the influential monographs published in the *Valori Plastici* series. Casorati participated in the Novecento exhibitions but he remained aloof from Margherita Sarfatti's movement, and in 1935 his studio hosted the "First Collective Exhibition of Italian Abstract Art," which included works by Lucio Fontana, Osvaldo Licini, and Fausto Melotti (see chapter 29). In the end, his pictures are more fundamentally modern, both in their psychological dimension and in their uncompromising emphasis on formal values, than anything produced by Sironi or Carrà, and they point up the falsity of a simplistic division between modernity and figurative painting.

The work of Giorgio Morandi is particularly important in this regard, for no other Italian artist remained so committed to a tradition-bound means of expression. His still lifes underwent major shifts of style, shedding the formal vocabulary of Metaphysical painting, with which Morandi had been associated in the teens (see chapter 27), to concentrate on the more purely formal concerns of the genre as defined by Cézanne, but at no point is there a wavering of purpose or intent. Like his contemporaries, Morandi studied Italian art of the past—from Giotto and Piero della Francesca (whose pale palette of blues and pinks he emulated) to Caravaggio and Fattori—but he was always alert to those specific qualities directly relevant to his craft. To de Chirico, Morandi seemed the quintessential Italian, who discovered in objects their "most consoling aspect, the eternal," while to a younger generation (the Strapaese, or "of the country") he epitomized the virtues of native Italian provincialism. His work has also been seen as an independent comment on the deteriorating politics of Fascist Italy, and his landscapes--the most beautiful to have been painted since the Macchiaioli—seem to proclaim eternal values in a time of uncertainty. In the context of the debates about art under the Fascist regime it is perhaps most important to note that Morandi continued to proclaim allegiance to a modernist aesthetic, on the one hand, and, on the other, promoted those humanistic values that have been among Italy's greatest legacy. The bottles and vases, teapots, and oil lamps that are the preferred objects of his still lifes, and the foothills of the Apennines, cultivated since antiquity, are transformed in his work into cultural totems.

Abstraction did not die under Fascism. Giacomo Balla, one of the original signatories of the *Manifesto of Futurist Painters* in 1910, and Enrico Prampolini remained committed to a Futurist vision (finally abandoned by Balla in the 1930s for a return to "absolute realism"). These two artist, together with Fortunato Depero, turned to mechanistic themes and expanded Futurism to the stage: Balla and Depero both designed sets for Diaghilev's Ballets Russes. "Everything is incisive, aristocratic, distinct. We are irresistibly attracted to the MECHANICAL SENSE, THE CLEAN, RESOLUTE. WE FEEL MECHANICALLY. WE FEEL MADE OF STEEL; WE TOO ARE MACHINES; WE TOO ARE MECHANIZED," they declared in a typically bombastic Futurist manifesto in 1922. Balla had pushed Futurism to abstraction, something Boccioni (not unlike Picasso), had resisted. Soon it was the airplane and Aeropainting (Aeropittura) that became their symbol of modernism. Between 1925 and 1937 Prampolini was based in Paris, where there was a considerable Italian community that included the Metaphysical circle of de Chirico, de Chirico's brother Alberto Savinio, and Filippo de Pisis, and where Picasso's Synthetic Cubist works were used to, in Prampolini's words, "transcend the transcription of visible reality . . . and launch ourselves toward the total equilibrium of the infinite, thereby giving life to images latent in a new world of cosmic reality." Following a trip to Paris in 1930–31, Licini, who had been associated with Futurism in its heroic age, painted his first abstract works. In 1931, Lucio Fontana held his first one-man show, and that same year he produced his colored cement tablets incised with a gestural abstraction. The center of activity for the new, international abstraction was the Galleria del Milione in Milan, where works by Josef Albers, Fernand Léger, Jean Arp, and others could be seen. The very existence of this gallery and the vitality of abstraction in the 1930s is an eloquent comment on the ineffectual efforts of Mussolini's ministers to impose a Fascist aesthetic.

Alberto Savinio (1891–1952)
Annunciation, 1932
Oil on canvas, 39 x 29½" (99 x 75 cm)
Civico Museo d'Arte Contemporanea, Palazzo Reale, Milan
Collection Boschi

Giorgio Morandi (1890–1964)
Still Life, 1929
Oil on canvas, 21⅝ x 22⅜" (55 x 58 cm)
Pinacoteca di Brera, Milan
Gift of Emilio and Maria Jesi

Filippo de Pisis (1896–1956)
Sacred Bread, 1930
Oil on canvas, 39 x 25⅝" (100 x 65 cm)
Private Collection

Giorgio Morandi (1890–1964)
Landscape, 1941
Oil on canvas
Private Collection, Milan

Mario Sironi (1885–1964)
Urban Architecture Composition,
ca. 1923
Oil on canvas, 23 x 32"
(58 x 80.3 cm)
Private Collection

OPPOSITE:
Felice Casorati (1886–1963)
Double Portrait (with Sister), 1924
Tempera on composite board,
48 x 36" (122 x 91 cm)
Private Collection

Renato Guttuso (1912–1987)
Execution in the Countryside, 1939
Oil on canvas, 39⅜ x 29½" (100 x 75 cm)
Galleria Nazionale d'Arte Moderna, Rome

OPPOSITE:
Enrico Prampolini (1894–1956)
The Everyday Automaton, 1930
Mixed media on canvas, 39⅜ x 21½" (100 x 80 cm)
Galleria Nazionale d'Arte Moderna, Rome

29.
Modernism and Beyond

Painting since World War II

In that remarkable and astonishingly concise treatise composed in 1435 by Leon Battista Alberti, already cited many times in this book, an idea of painting was put forward in deceptively simple terms. Alberti believed in painting as a counterfeit of nature: not simply as a test of artistic skills, but as a means of effectively communicating emotions and ideas. "The aim of the painter," he wrote, "is to obtain praise, favor and good-will for his work much more than riches. The painter will achieve this if his painting holds and moves the eyes and minds of spectators." For almost five hundred years, Alberti's views remained more or less intact, which is to say that although various artists or groups of artists experimented with the means by which these expressive goals could best be achieved, no one questioned the belief that the key to art was its affective power and that this ability to move viewers was intimately tied with the imitation of nature. Even the Divisionist Pellizza da Volpedo (see chapter 26) subscribed to this view, for he was bent on intensifying, not negating, the communicative powers of art. The Futurists (see chapter 27) sought to embody the dynamics of nature rather than to counterfeit her appearance, but they too would have subscribed to this aspect of Alberti's thought—however much they might have caviled the academic theory of idealism that can also be traced back to his treatise. Even the question of the creation of a Fascist art—of an art that could exemplify the ideals of the State—was one Alberti could have imagined, and so also was the quest of Renato Guttuso to effect the way people react to events through his violent, expressionist brushwork (see chapter 28). Although early twentieth-century painting is usually seen as marking an irreversible break with the past, in these respects that generalization is false. Indeed, from the standpoint of late-twentieth-century painting, Picasso and Boccioni, Chagall and de Chirico seem to have as much in common with the art of the old masters as they do with what followed.

When, however, one of the key figures of postwar Italian art, Piero Manzoni, declared in 1960 that, "A picture has value in that it exists: there is no need to say anything; being is all that matters: two colors in harmony, or two shades of the same color, already represent a relationship which is extraneous to the meaning of the unique, limitless, absolutely dynamic surface," the notion of what art is and what relation it has to the needs of humanity—a major Albertian theme—was altered in a fundamental way. It is questionable whether anyone prior to the twentieth century reduced the quest of painting to the problem of how "to produce a totally white—or rather, totally colorless—surface removed from all pictorial phenomena . . . a white which is in no sense a polar landscape, an evocation or even merely a beautiful material, a sensation or a symbol, or anything else of the kind; a white surface which is a white surface and nothing else . . . : being."

Compared to Manzoni's achromes (that is, colorless pictures)—which, in fact, possess a remarkably sensuous beauty—the symbolic-abstract work of Osvaldo Licini and the slashed and punctured canvases of Lucio Fontana, with their attempt to push the spatial investigations of Futurism into a new, more esoteric realm by, quite literally, breaking through the picture plane, seem burdened with the linguistics and rhetoric of a past age.

The battles of postwar painting have been and continue to be fought not so much over matters of morality, the rights of an oppressed minority, the issue of a national identity, or one or another philosophies of life (all of crucial interest to nineteenth- and early twentieth-century art); nor even over the question of modernity. Rather, the battles have been over the artist's creative nature; over art as a means of individual expression; and over art as something self-defining, in which any artistic action represents an act of interference. One cannot help but note here that at the end of the 1930s, following their lifelong commitment to modernism, the old Futurists Giacomo Balla and Osvaldo Licini turned their backs on abstraction. Balla went so far as to declare that, "pure art is to be found in absolute realism, without which one falls into decorative, ornamental forms," while Licini, a dedicated Communist, created his own mythological world.

The Gruppo Origine, founded in 1951 by Alberto Burri together with Ettore Colla, Mario Ballocco, and Giuseppe Capogrossi, renounced both spatial illusionism and descriptive color, without which a widely accessible visual language is not possible. Burri's stitched sackcloth pieces replaced representation with a dialogue of materials—without, however, in any way minimizing the factor of a self-willed composition and, hence, a pictorial intention. Burri began painting while in a prisoner-of-war camp in Texas in the mid-1940s (he returned to Italy in 1946), and the resemblance of his compositions in sackcloth and wood to the painted canvases of Franz Kline is real, not casual, however different their effects.

In 1967, the critic Germano Celant organized a group show in Genoa under the name Arte Povera, a term indicating a linguistic process by which the signs of language are reduced to archetypes. This is, in effect, what Pino Pascali accomplished with great wit in his canvas of an antique stone wall, the material being identified by the stenciled word *pietra* (stone). There is an obvious parallel to the play on words and surfaces Jasper Johns explored in his target and map paintings of these same years, reminding us that the line of exchange that had, before World War I, linked Milan and Paris, now extended to New York. And yet, Pascali's picture has a very different effect from those by Jasper Johns, not only because it renounces color, but because the blocks of stones it refers to carry a cultural allusion to ancient architecture. In his canvas, representational illusionism is spoofed within a particular cultural context.

Arte Povera was not a unified movement. Michelangelo Pistoletto, who was included in the Arte Povera exhibition of 1968 in Bologna, had, in 1962, painted blurred figures on the surface of a mirror, thereby combining reflections of a reality in flux (the viewers in the room reflected in the mirror) with the frozen images of art. One wonders if he knew the seventeenth-century painted mirrors in the Colonna palace in Rome, with their sumptuous vases of flowers painted by Mario dei Fiori and their flying putti by Carlo Maratta, which were, however, a game of illusionism rather than, in Pistoletto's words, an attempt to "make the laws of objective reality enter the painting." To no less a degree than Pascali, Pistoletto reduced painting to an esoteric idea. Later, Pistoletto combined a cast of a classical sculpture with a pile of rags, appropriating conflicting, cultural symbols. This is only superficially related to the enigmatic juxtapositions found in the Metaphysical paintings of de Chirico (see chapter 27), in which the world created on canvas is self-contained and expresses a coherent, artistic vision.

Mimmo Rotella found in the peeling poster advertisements of movie stars applied in layers to the walls of Rome a ready-made image of society that required only a few gestural tears in the surface to carry the artist's voice, which seems in these works to almost disappear behind the onslaught of a foreign culture whose pop heroes are Elvis Presley and Marilyn Monroe. The glittering society these mutilated artifacts evoke is *La Dolce Vita* of Federico Fellini, with its concomitant feeling of alienation.

With the economic miracle of the 1960s, Italy became a modern industrial power with an unprecedented rapidity. In the wake of the student strikes and demonstrations of 1968, Italian painting freed itself of its attachment to events in America and of an elaborate conceptualism. The movement was the Transavanguardia, and its protagonists, Sandro Chia, Enzo Cucchi, Mimmo Paladino, Francesco Clemente, and Nicola De Maria, were all born after 1945 and came of age in the 1960s. If their pictures have anything in common, it is a new dialogue with the past and the reemergence of the personality of the artist. It might be the witty, playful personality of Chia, whose athletic figures seem at times to leap free of the classical moorings of the frescoes and canvases of Michelangelo, Titian, and Tintoretto, "the heroes of my childhood . . . [who] . . . I'll . . . make dance on only one leg to my music and for my pleasure." At other times, it is the homoerotic revelations of Clemente, sometimes filtered in an ironic vein through recollections of figures of the infant Christ and Saint John or some allegorical work by a Renaissance master. Paladino's enigmatic allegories make references to a whole range of sources, from cave painting to African masks, purposely camouflaging any clear meaning—just as de Chirico had found in the enigma his power of expression. Cucchi's *Picture in the Dark by the Sea* is a nightmarish vision of abandonment and death. In many respects, these works seem less "modern" than the work of the conceptual artists of the 1960s, and indeed the term *transavanguardia* suggests a desire to go beyond modernity. But toward what?

When Aeneas arrived in Carthage on his way to Rome, he cautiously wandered into the city and happened upon the Temple of Juno, where he found a depiction of the Trojan War. "For the first time," writes Vergil, "his fears were allayed, and for the first time he dared to hope for life and to feel some confidence in spite of his distress. . . . It was only a picture, but sighing deeply he let his thoughts feed on it, and his face was wet with tears." The ability to communicate in elevated terms and to "move the hearts and minds of spectators" has stood at the center of Italian painting since its inception two thousand five hundred years ago, and it is this heritage—asserted by Aristotle, Horace, and Pliny, and reaffirmed by Alberti, Vasari, and Bellori—that poses a daunting challenge to Italian artists today.

Alberto Burri (1915–)
Sackcloth 1953, 1953
Burlap, sewn, patched, and
glued, over canvas
33⅞ x 39⅜" (86.04 x 100.01 cm)
The Museum of Modern Art,
New York
Mr. and Mrs. David M. Solinger Fund

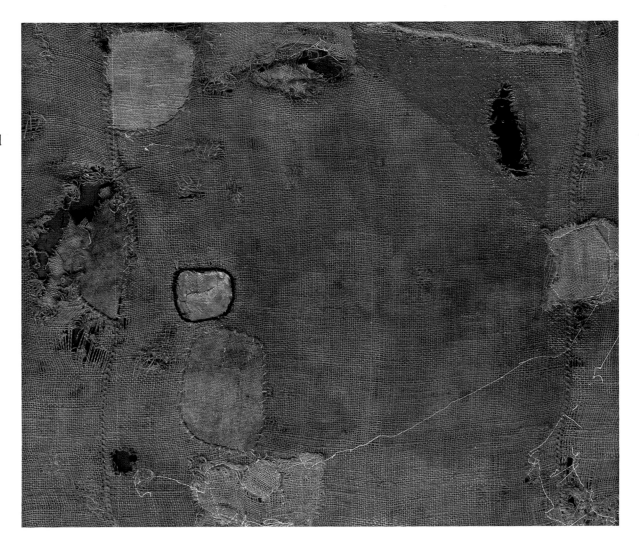

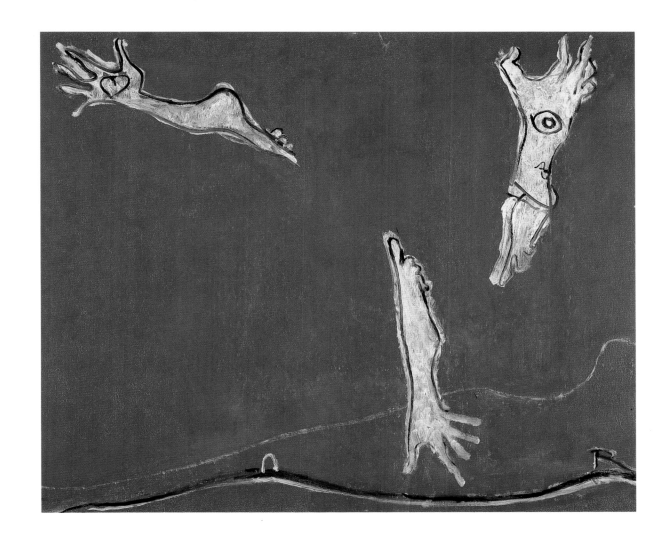

Osvaldo Licini (1894–1958)
Amalassunta No. 2, 1952
Oil on canvas, 31½ x 39⅜"
(80 x 100 cm)
Galleria Nazionale d'Arte Moderna,
Rome

Lucio Fontana (1899–1968)
Spatial Concept—Expectations, 1959
Water-based paint and oil on canvas
65¾ x 50" (167 x 127 cm)
Musée d'Art Moderne de la Ville de Paris

Piero Manzoni (1933–1963)
Achrome, 1959
Canvas and kaolin, 39⅜ x 31 ⁵⁄₁₆" (100 x 79.5 cm)
Private Collection

OPPOSITE:
Mimmo Rotella (1918–)
The Assault, 1963
Collage on canvas, 59½ x 53½" (151 x 136 cm)
Staatsgalerie, Stuttgart

Sandro Chia (1946–)
The Water Bearer, 1981
Oil on canvas, 81⅛ x 67" (206 x 170 cm)
The Tate Gallery, London

OPPOSITE TOP:
Enzo Cucchi (1949–)
Picture in the Dark by the Sea, 1980
Oil on canvas, 81⅛ x 140½" (206 x 357 cm)
Galerie Bruno Bischofberger, Zurich

OPPOSITE BOTTOM:
Mimmo Paladino (1948–)
Untitled, 1982
Oil on canvas, 78¾ x 118⅛" (200 x 300 cm)
Nationalgalerie, Staatliche Museen, Berlin

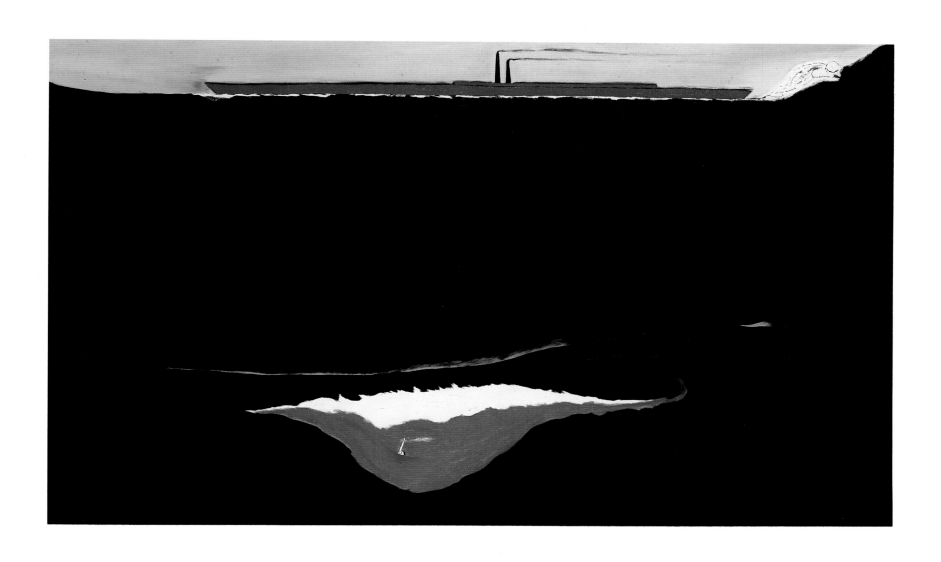

Francesco Clemente (1952–)
Broken Hearts, 1990
Pigment on linen, 52 x 44" (132 x 112 cm)
Courtesy Sperone Westwater Gallery, New York

Index

Page numbers in italic denote illustrations.